The Economics
of the
Davis-Bacon Act

The Economics of the Davis-Bacon Act

An Analysis of Prevailing-Wage Laws

John P. Gould and George Bittlingmayer

American Enterprise Institute for Public Policy Research
Washington, D.C.

John P. Gould is professor of economics at the Graduate School of Business of the University of Chicago. He served as special assistant for economic affairs to the secretary of labor from 1969 to 1970.

George Bittlingmayer is a graduate student in the Department of Economics at the University of Chicago and a lecturer at Northeastern Illinois University.

Portions of this study originally appeared in a slightly different form in John P. Gould, *Davis-Bacon Act: The Economics of Prevailing Wage Laws,* Special Analysis No. 15 (Washington, D.C.: American Enterprise Institute, 1971).

Library of Congress Cataloging in Publication Data

Gould, John P   1939–
    The economics of the Davis-Bacon act.

    (AEI studies ; 278)
    1. Wages—Construction workers—United States.   I. Bittlingmayer, George, joint author.   II. Title.   III. Series: American Enterprise Institute for Public Policy Research.   AEI studies ; 278.

KF3505.C65G69   344.73′01289   80-11484
ISBN 0-8447-3381-4

AEI Studies 278

Printed in the United States of America

CONTENTS

1
Introduction

The Davis-Bacon Act requires payment of "prevailing" wages and fringe benefits to workers who are employed in the construction of federal government buildings or public works. The required wage rates are determined by the secretary of labor to be prevailing in the city, town, village, or other civil subdivision of the state in which the work is performed. Numerous other laws incorporate the Davis-Bacon prevailing-wage requirement for federally assisted projects such as highways, airports, housing, hospitals, and schools. This study surveys the literature dealing with the economic and social consequences of this legislation, paying particular attention to its influence on construction industry wages and on the cost of projects covered by it.

Why should a law requiring the payment of prevailing wages be suspected of contributing to unnecessary increases in construction costs and of adversely affecting the structure of wages in the construction industry? The economic analysis of Chapter 4 indicates that two factors taken together tend to raise significantly the cost of construction that is covered by the act. First, the construction industry labor market has, in effect, two prevailing wage rates. One applies to open-shop firms and is arrived at in the same way as most other wages and prices in the economy. Workers enter or leave this sector of the construction-industry labor market—causing wages to fall or rise—in response to changes in economy-wide wage levels, and in response to other factors, such as the fraction of the time they expect to be laid off, the hazards of the job, and the amount of training required. The other, higher rate is the union rate, which typically runs 30 to 70 percent above the rate in the open-shop sector. These rates are higher because the unions stand in what may be regarded as a monopoly position in relation to a large fraction of local contractors, in particular those who have relatively large operations based in urban areas and those engaged in nonresidential construction. Unions are in a position to demand and obtain higher wages from these employers, and these higher wages result in higher construction costs.

The second factor in the set of circumstances that makes the Davis-Bacon Act costly is the character of Department of Labor wage determinations. As a result of the department's procedural rules and what can only be taken as the pro-union bias of the wage determination staff, the wage determinations tend to represent disproportionately the union-negotiated rates, often from areas other than those in which the work is being done—despite the clear legal requirement that local rates must be used. Consequently, open-shop contractors are confronted with the choice of either paying their workers substantially higher wages during the time they work on projects covered by the act or not bidding at all. Either way, in the many instances in which open-shop contractors would otherwise be able to perform the work for less, wage determinations imposed by the Department of Labor result in extra project costs on the order of 5 to 15 percent.

Obviously, the law would tend to have little effect in areas where most construction workers belong to unions. In most cases, contractors would be paying the higher union rates whether or not the Department of Labor specified them. In many other areas this is not the case, however. The percentage of the construction labor force that is unionized varies considerably from one area to another. But, as the Labor Department regulations stand at present, the union rates become the prevailing rates if as little as 30 percent of the workers in a given skill category are union members. Typically, the negotiated rates for the different building trades are uniform in an area. The open-shop rates, however, vary among contractors and may even vary among the workers of a given trade employed by a single contractor. Labor Department regulations state, however, that the *exact* rate prevailing among 30 percent of the members of a given trade in an area may be taken as the prevailing rate for the whole category. The result, documented in numerous instances by the General Accounting Office and others, is that the wage determination reflects the highest wage rates paid in a locality rather than the average or "prevailing" rate.

The rules, when faithfully followed, result in a bias in wage-rate determinations. Yet there is considerable evidence that the department's own regulations are consistently violated in a manner that imparts an additional upward bias in a large number of cases. The act itself states clearly, and the legislative history supports the interpretation, that *local* rates are to be used. Yet, in determinations for many projects being built outside metropolitan areas, local rates are not used. Instead, the rates from neighboring large cities, reflecting the greater unionization and higher living costs of major urban centers, are held to be the rates that should be paid on such projects.

Ironically, the effect is often exactly what the original framers of the act claimed they wanted to avoid. In the cases where "imported" rates are used, local construction work is performed not by local labor and local contractors paying the locally prevailing wages, but rather by workers and firms from the metropolitan area whose wage rates formed the basis for the wage determination in the first place. Projects done this way cost more than they would if performed by local labor, and the primary social objectives of the act are not met. In fact, the displacement of local by imported labor is one of the chief results.

The annual cost of the Davis-Bacon Act is probably on the order of several hundred million, and perhaps as high as a billion, dollars. This estimate includes both the direct costs to government of increased wage payments as well as the considerable administrative costs borne by government and contractors operating under the act. In addition, the act tends to enlarge the share of total construction activity undertaken by workers who are members of trade unions.

While the direct economic consequences are increased construction costs, less obvious social consequences also stem from the act. Along with negotiated rates of pay considerably higher than those prevailing in open-shop employment, union agreements contain extensive restrictions on hiring and employment practices. These restrictions define the categories of employment, in particular limiting the use of workers who are not full journeymen. Open-shop firms often employ less experienced workers as journeymen helpers or trainees, whereas union rules for the most part restrict the less experienced workers to apprenticeship status. Although rates of pay for the open-shop categories are flexible, in union shops apprenticeship rates are set at about half the journeymen rates.

More importantly, admission to union apprenticeship programs registered with the Department of Labor is largely controlled by the unions. These apprenticeship programs have historically had a disproportionately small number of blacks and members of other minority groups. Open-shop firms, on the other hand, provide greater opportunities for on-the-job training and flexibility in work assignments. Consequently, a laborer or helper has the opportunity to perform tasks that are often restricted to special trades in union shops. To the extent that work covered by the act goes disproportionately to union shops or to open shops that must operate under union-shop categories and wage rates, the effect is to decrease minority and youth employment in construction.

Various remedies are possible. The Department of Labor could change its wage-determination procedure to reflect better the actual wages paid in an area. It should be noted, however, that simply taking the average of wage rates paid might still result in a determination substantially above the open-shop rate. In many cases this would still result in open-shop contractors declining to bid on covered work. Nor would a change in procedures for wage determinations address the problem of what job classifications should be recognized. It has been suggested that wage determinations be made only for one category of worker: unskilled laborers. This would greatly reduce the workload on the Labor Department staff and would provide, as well, a minimum wage for workers who might be regarded as most vulnerable to wage cutting. It is questionable, however, whether, in the context of today's economy, even such protection is necessary.

The likelihood that the Department of Labor will ever change the wage-determination procedure in this fashion is slight, however. Despite frequent promises to change the procedure during the last ten to twenty years, the Department of Labor has persisted in making wage determinations that violate both the letter and the intent of the law, that harm the economic well-being of large numbers of workers, and that increase the cost of government to the taxpayer. The best solution from the standpoint of economic and social policy would undoubtedly be to repeal the Davis-Bacon Act altogether.

2
The Legislative Framework

The Davis-Bacon Act was enacted in 1931 to compel contractors performing construction work for the federal government to pay their workers the wage "prevailing" in the community in which the construction takes place. Amendments to the act added "prevailing" fringe benefits to the definition of prevailing wages and charged the secretary of labor with the responsibility of determining in advance the wages acceptable on federal projects. The Davis-Bacon Act represented a dramatic reversal of earlier federal policy, which had attempted to secure completion of federal projects at the lowest possible cost to the tax-paying public.

Many laws have also been passed that include Davis-Bacon prevailing-wage-determination provisions for federally assisted projects, although the federal government itself is not party to the contracts for such projects. As will be shown in the next chapter, there has been a tendency for the Department of Labor to make inappropriately high determinations of the prevailing wage in a number of cases. This policy has had unfortunate consequences that tend to defeat the main purpose of many of the laws that embody Davis-Bacon prevailing-wage clauses.

The Legislative History of the Davis-Bacon Act

Prevailing-wage legislation was not a new concept in 1931, when the Davis-Bacon Act was introduced and passed.[1] Various states, beginning

---

[1] Background on the Davis-Bacon Act may be obtained from the following sources: Associated General Contractors of America, *Davis-Bacon Handbook* (Washington, D.C.: Associated General Contractors of America, 1977); Armand J. Thieblot, Jr., *The Davis-Bacon Act*, Labor Relations and Public Policy Series, Report No. 10 (Philadelphia: University of Pennsylvania Press, 1975); U.S. Gen-

with Kansas in 1891, had passed similar legislation requiring workmen on state-funded projects to be paid prevailing wages. Five states had passed such legislation by 1931, and twenty-one had done so by 1935. By 1978 all but nine states had passed "little Davis-Bacon Acts." Their provisions vary, but in each case they stipulate that contractors performing construction for the state must pay their workers some "current" or "prevailing" wage.

The passage of forty-one similar state laws over a period of nearly eighty years indicates that prevailing-wage legislation was not exclusively a product of the economic circumstances of the Depression, although those circumstances appear to have contributed to its passage at the federal level. Robert J. Bacon of New York attempted to introduce federal prevailing-wage legislation as early as 1927. Between 1927 and 1931, as the economy slowed, fourteen attempts were made to introduce prevailing-wage legislation for federal construction projects.

The attempts to get such legislation passed seem to have been sparked by the practice of some contractors of importing workers from low-wage areas, chiefly the South, to do construction work on projects located in northern states. Contractors operating in this fashion were often able to underbid contractors using local labor, and the charge was made that local workers lost employment as a result. Senator Bacon described this view in highly emotional language during debate on the bill:

> A practice has been growing up in carrying out the building program where certain itinerant, irresponsible contractors, with itinerant, cheap, bootleg labor, have been going around throughout the country "picking" off a contract here, and a contract there, and local labor and local contractors have been standing on the sidelines looking in. Bitterness has been caused in many communities because of this situation.
>
> This bill, my friends, is simply to give local labor and the local contractor a fair opportunity to participate in this building program.
>
> I think it is a fair proposition where the Government is building these post offices and public buildings throughout the country that the local contractor and local labor may have

eral Accounting Office, *The Davis-Bacon Act Should Be Repealed*, 1979; U.S. Department of Labor, Division of Wage Determinations, Office of the Solicitor, *The Legislative History of the Davis-Bacon Act*, 1962; and U.S. Library of Congress, Congressional Research Service, *The Davis-Bacon Act: History, Administration, Pro and Con Arguments, and Congressional Proposals*, prepared by Joseph F. Fulton, July 11, 1978.

a "fair break" in getting the contract. If the local contractor is successful in obtaining the bid, it means that local labor will be employed because that local contractor is going to continue in business in that community after the work is done. If an outside contractor gets the contract, and there is no discrimination against the honest contractor, it means that he will have to pay the prevailing wages, just like the local contractor.[2]

Evidence exists, however, which indicates that more than local employment was at stake. Congressman Thomas L. Blanton of Texas commented during discussion on the bill that "if this bill were not demanded by organized labor it would not have a chance of passage in this House under suspension of the rules."[3] By stipulating that the prevailing wage be paid in a heavily unionized area, it becomes much less likely that a nonunion contractor based outside the area and paying his workers less would find it profitable to compete there. At the time the final bill was under consideration, the American Federation of Labor and its affiliates had endorsed it.

It should be noted that the Associated General Contractors of America was in favor of a modified bill that would have allowed wage rates to be determined in advance by the governmental department contracting for the work. Its endorsement of such a measure was perhaps due to three factors: a desire to keep government projects from fly-by-night nonmembers; a feeling that under the circumstances a modified bill was the best it could hope to achieve; and a belief that this measure might stop the decline in prices that the construction industry was experiencing as a result of the Depression. This last interpretation is supported by the way the association qualified its support of the bill: "[T]his association is in favor of the Government contractors paying the local prevailing rate of wages *during this emergency*."[4] The request that wage rates be determined in advance was later incorporated into an amendment to the bill.

Evidence presented during discussion of the bill in Congress also indicates that the practice of using nonlocal labor for federal projects may not have been widespread. For twenty-six Treasury Department projects employing 1,724 workers, only 368 workers were found to have been from outside the area in which the project was located. Outside workers were commonly employed on projects in such cities

---

[2] Department of Labor, *Legislative History*, p. 1.

[3] U.S. Congress, House, *Congressional Record*, vol. 74, 71st Congress, 3d session, February 28, 1931, p. 6508.

[4] Ibid. Emphasis added.

as Boise, Idaho; Fargo, North Dakota; and Juneau, Alaska, where large supplies of construction labor were not available. Projects in such cities as San Francisco, Milwaukee, and Memphis had few if any outside employees.[5]

Moreover, at least part of the resentment against construction performed by itinerant contractors using migratory labor seems to have been motivated by racism. Congressman Miles Clayton Allgood of Alabama put the matter most directly:

> Reference has been made to a contractor from Alabama who went to New York with bootleg labor. That is a fact. That contractor has cheap colored labor that he transports, and he puts them in cabins, and it is labor of that sort that is in competition with white labor throughout the country.[6]

Although other legislators were not as forthright as Congressman Allgood, the issue was alluded to at several other points during discussion of the bill, as in New York Congressman Fiorello LaGuardia's discussion of the construction of a Veteran's Bureau hospital:

> I saw with my own eyes the labor that he [the contractor] imported from the South and the conditions under which they were working. These unfortunate men were huddled in shacks living under the most wretched conditions and being paid wages far below the standard. These unfortunate men were being exploited by the contractor. Local skilled and unskilled labor were not employed. The workmanship of the cheap imported labor was of course very inferior.[7]

It is not clear from the evidence whether the practice of using black labor from the South was common. It did receive some attention in the press, and legislators may have felt that unless measures were undertaken, it would become more common. Since federal construction was a large fraction of total construction during the Depression, a prevailing-wage law for federal construction would probably have sharply reduced the employment of black workers in construction.

It should be mentioned that black workers imported from the South would almost certainly have earned more at their new jobs than at their previous employment. It is clear from the discussion of the bill that the legislators' intention, insofar as the problem of

---

[5] Decision of General J. R. McCarl, comptroller general of the United States, January 10, 1931, in ibid., p. 6506.

[6] House, *Congressional Record*, vol. 74, p. 6513.

[7] Ibid., p. 6510.

itinerant laborers existed, was to keep these relatively well-paying jobs from such laborers.

The original act, passed on March 3, 1931, required that contractors performing construction, alterations, and repair of federal buildings for amounts in excess of $5,000 pay their workmen at least the prevailing wage for work of a similar nature in the city, town, village, or other civil subdivision in which the buildings were located. The act was very brief and poorly conceived. Complaints were made almost immediately by contractors who wanted the prevailing wage to be determined in advance. They argued that it was difficult to bid on a project without sure knowledge of the Department of Labor's wage determination. The unions, on the other hand, did not want rates to be predetermined, fearing that an unfriendly administration might set low rates. They did complain, however, that the law, as it stood, could not be effectively enforced.

In the amendment that passed in 1935, both groups obtained satisfaction. Wage rates were henceforth predetermined by the secretary of labor, and an enforcement mechanism was adopted. The contracting officer was allowed to withhold payment and terminate the contract, and the comptroller general was allowed to disburse from the withheld funds any wages that workers should have received but did not. In addition, the threshold was lowered from $5,000 to $2,000; painting, decorating, and public works projects were added; and contractors were required to pay wages at least once a week, regardless of any other provisions the contractor and employee might have made. The next major change in the act occurred in 1964, when it was amended to include fringe benefits such as medical and hospital care and pensions. (The amended act is reprinted as Appendix C.)

State Prevailing-Wage Legislation and Unionization

The pattern of prevailing-wage laws in more than forty states supports the view that such legislation favors organized labor. Only nine states have no such law. As Table 1 shows, these states all have a lower percentage of unionized nonagricultural employment than the United States as a whole. Whether or not a state has a right-to-work law serves as an additional indication of the influence of unionized labor. Although only eighteen out of fifty states had such laws in 1974, eight out of the nine states without prevailing-wage laws had right-to-work laws, Vermont being the exception. These figures strongly support the belief that prevailing-wage laws are special-interest measures.

TABLE 1

UNIONIZED NONAGRICULTURAL EMPLOYMENT
IN STATES WITHOUT PREVAILING-WAGE LEGISLATION, 1974

	Unionized Nonagricultural Employment (percent)
States[a]	
Georgia	14.5
Iowa	21.2
Mississippi	12.0
North Carolina	6.9
North Dakota	15.1
South Carolina	8.0
South Dakota	11.0
Vermont	17.7
Virginia	13.8
United States	26.2

[a] The list of states is from the U.S. General Accounting Office, *The Davis-Bacon Act Should Be Repealed*, 1979, Appendix XVI (reply of the Department of Labor to the GAO study), p. 238.

SOURCE: U.S. Bureau of the Census, *Statistical Abstract of the United States, 1978*, Table No. 699, p. 430.

Other Federal Laws Requiring Prevailing-Wage Determinations

The Davis-Bacon Act itself only requires that contractors pay wages as determined by the secretary of labor for "every contract in excess of $2,000 to which the United States or the District of Columbia is a party, for construction, alteration, and/or repair, including painting and decorating, of public buildings or public works of the United States or the District of Columbia." Not covered, for example, are highway construction, the construction of public housing, or the construction of buildings that the federal government funds in whole or in part but that are operated by state or local governments. However, subsequent laws authorizing expenditures for such projects have often included clauses specifying that Davis-Bacon wage rates be paid. In 1965, twenty-four federal laws required Davis-Bacon wage determinations; in 1975, sixty-three; and in 1977, seventy-seven. (The seventy-seven statutes are listed in Appendix D.) The Federal-Aid Highway Act of 1956, for example, incorporates a prevailing-wage clause, as do the Solid Waste Disposal Act, the Health Professions

Educational Assistance Act of 1963, and the Housing and Urban Development Acts of 1965 and 1970. According to the General Accounting Office, in 1977 construction amounting to $37.8 billion was covered under the Davis-Bacon Act and under the laws that invoke its provisions.[8]

Summary

The Davis-Bacon Act was ostensibly passed to prevent itinerant contractors from using laborers from low-wage areas of the country to undertake federal construction projects in high-wage areas. It is doubtful whether this practice, which is uncommon today, was in fact ever widespread. The impetus for prevailing-wage legislation seems to have come from other sources. It is particularly difficult to sustain the belief that the function of the Davis-Bacon Act is to prevent construction contracts from going to itinerant contractors, since local contractors are nearly unanimous in their desire to see Davis-Bacon repealed. The enactment of prevailing-wage legislation in many states suggests that other factors may be more important. In 1978 only nine states did not have such legislation. The prevailing-wage laws in the remaining forty-one were passed as early as 1891. The suspicion that such laws tend to benefit organized labor is strongly supported by the fact that the nine states without state prevailing-wage legislation have unusually low rates of unionization.

In addition, considerable federal legislation requiring Davis-Bacon determinations for categories of work not provided for in the original act has also been passed. This may be interpreted either as evidence that Congress continues to find wage protection a necessary legislative goal, or as a continuing testament to the political influence of organized labor. The accumulated evidence on who benefits from Davis-Bacon wage determinations indicates that the second interpretation is more likely correct. The real significance of prevailing-wage legislation, then, is the great increase it imposes on the cost of construction. It also increases the employment opportunities of high-wage workers, while decreasing the opportunities of those paid less.

It should also be noted that the Davis-Bacon Act and the 1935 amendment that gave it the fundamental form it has today were passed before the first federal minimum-wage legislation. It is difficult to argue that Davis-Bacon provides basic wage protection to construction workers. Although unemployment is high among construction workers,

---

[8] General Accounting Office, *Davis-Bacon Act*, p. 3.

this is largely a result of the greater fluctuations in construction activity and is compensated for by the payment of high wages (as will be seen in the next chapter). The effect of the act, to the degree that it is successful in artificially raising wages in an industry in which wages are already high, is to increase unemployment in that industry even further. Most of the workers for whom wage determinations are made are skilled craftsmen earning above-average wages. To the degree that the act is successful in placing a lower boundary on wages paid to workers fortunate enough to be employed in work that falls under the act, the effect is to provide such workers with a minimum income, and a rather high one at that.

3

Administration of the Davis-Bacon Act

Two types of prevailing-wage rates are established by the Department of Labor (DOL): area rates and project rates. Until recently only determinations for specific projects were made, but the burden of making a large number of determinations led to an administrative change permitting area determinations that would cover more than one project. The Labor Department staff has not been allocated the resources, however, to conduct even the reduced number of determinations that the modified procedure allows. The result has been that prevailing wages are often determined improperly. In some cases wage rates from noncontiguous areas have been applied; in other cases the wage schedules of union-negotiated wage contracts were simply adopted as the prevailing schedule, despite the existence of a considerable non-union sector. Administrative rules stipulating that the exact wage that is paid to 30 percent or more of the workers in a given classification be considered the prevailing wage have in particular led to the adoption of union-negotiated wage rates as the prevailing wage.

Contractors who find themselves unable to bid on a project because the determined wages are higher than they customarily pay do have recourse to an appeals procedure, but that procedure is cumbersome and costly. Also, a successful appeal does not mean that the contractor who pays the cost of the appeal will win the contract. There is, then, practically no incentive for any contractor to appeal an inappropriately high set of minimum-wage determinations for a project.

Procedure for Predetermination of Wage Rates

The procedure for predetermination of prevailing wages was formalized in a directive from the secretary of labor in December 1963.[1]

---

[1] These directives are contained in U.S. Office of the Federal Register, *Code of Federal Regulations*, 1978, Title 29, Part 1.

It applies to the Davis-Bacon Act and to many other acts, as well as to "such other statutes as may, from time to time, confer upon the secretary of labor similar wage determining authority." The secretary's regulations define the prevailing wage as follows:

> (1) The rate of wages paid in the area in which the work is to be performed, to the majority of those employed in that classification in construction in the area similar to the proposed undertaking;
> (2) In the event that there is not a majority paid at the same rate, then the rate paid to the greater number; *Provided,* Such greater number constitutes 30 percent of those employed; or
> (3) In the event that less than 30 percent of those so employed receive the same rate, then the average rate.[2]

The secretary of labor has delegated the authority to administer the act to the assistant secretary of labor for employment standards. The assistant secretary determines rates for such projects as buildings, bridges, dams, highways, tunnels, sewers, power lines, railways, airports (buildings and runways), apartment houses, wharves, levees, canals, dredging, land clearing, and excavating.[3] This list is by no means exhaustive. Furthermore, when one considers that there are over 3,000 civil subdivisions in the United States, and that any one project may employ workers in twenty or thirty classifications, it becomes clear that keeping track of the "prevailing wage" is a considerable task.

The types of information considered in making determinations include:

> (1) Statements showing wage rates paid on projects. . . .
> (2) Signed collective bargaining agreements. . . .
> (3) Wage rates determined for public construction by state and local officials pursuant to prevailing wage legislation.
> (4) Information furnished by federal and state agencies. . . .
> (5) Any other information pertinent to the determination of prevailing wage rates.[4]

Other pertinent information includes field surveys conducted in the area of the proposed project for the purpose of obtaining sufficient information upon which to make a determination.

---

[2] Ibid., p. 18.
[3] Ibid., p. 19.
[4] Ibid.

Section 1.8 of Title 29 of the *Code of Federal Regulations* contains two other relevant provisions:

> (a) In making a wage-rate determination, projects completed more than one year prior to the date of request for the determination may, but need not, be considered.
>
> (b) If there has been no similar construction within the area in the past year, wage rates paid on the nearest similar construction may be considered.[5]

While these conditions are explicit about many aspects of the procedure for prevailing-wage determinations, much discretion is still necessary. In practice, it appears that a disproportionately large number of wage determinations carry union wages regardless of area or type of construction. This is often a consequence of the "majority" rule, the "30 percent" rule, and the Section 1.8 authorization of determinations on the basis of the "nearest similar construction." Typically, union rates for a given classification are the same for all union workers in an area, while nonunion rates vary from contractor to contractor and even among workers doing similar work for the same firm. The bias in favor of union rates is also likely to be a consequence of the very large number of determinations that have to be made each year and of the resulting pressure for expeditious determinations.

The Administrative Burden of Wage Determinations on Government

During the first years of the Davis-Bacon Act, only project determinations were made. In 1946, for example, 4,453 wage determinations were issued. By 1963 this number had risen to 46,397, and revised Department of Labor procedures allowed general or area determinations to be made in areas that had considerable construction coming under Davis-Bacon provisions. During fiscal 1977, DOL's Division of Construction Wage Determinations issued 15,674 project determinations and 2,257 general determinations.[6] A single determination requires anywhere from 10 to 300 job classifications—100 classifications per determination is not at all unusual. The yearly cost to the government in administering the act was placed at $12.4 million for 1977 by the General Accounting Office (GAO).[7]

---

[5] Ibid., p. 21.

[6] U.S. Library of Congress, Congressional Research Service, *The Davis-Bacon Act, History, Administration, Pro and Con Arguments, and Congressional Proposals*, prepared by Joseph F. Fulton, July 11, 1978, p. 16.

[7] U.S. General Accounting Office, *The Davis-Bacon Act Should Be Repealed*, 1979, p. 83.

In 1967 Secretary of Labor W. Willard Wirtz said in a letter to Henry Eschwege of GAO:

> Determining wage rates under the Davis-Bacon Act for residential construction has been a troublesome problem and will continue to be a problem so long as the Department of Labor lacks adequate facilities for collecting wage information in various parts of the country. As you know, wage rates in the construction industry in any area vary from time to time, and up-to-date information is essential. The Department of Labor currently [1967] has a staff of 70 persons engaged in wage determining here in Washington and, also, 5 field representatives handling special matters as required. *These are not nearly enough for accurate determinations,* particularly in the residential field.[8]

Three years later, in another review of inappropriately high wage determinations, GAO noted that, by January 1970, the Labor Department still had not increased the wage determination staff, contrary to the expressed intent of Secretary Wirtz in 1967.[9]

A former employee of the Division of Wage Determinations interviewed in 1974 said that, typically, "the rate determination procedure was automatic."[10] The division relied on signed union contracts in large part because inadequate funding precluded further staff work. "In many cases, halfhearted mail surveys were the only thing attempted, and then the union rate was fallen back on when the response was too low."[11] Although various administrative measures have been taken to ease the burden of construction wage determinations on the Department of Labor, such as the adoption of area determinations and the use of data processing equipment (determinations were handled manually until 1979), examples of improper wage determinations abound in studies as recent as GAO's 1979 examination of DOL's administration of the act.[12]

---

[8] U.S. General Accounting Office, *Need for More Realistic Minimum Wage Rate Determinations for Certain Federally Financed Housing in Washington Metropolitan Area,* 1968. Emphasis added.

[9] U.S. General Accounting Office, *Construction Costs for Certain Federally Financed Housing Projects Increased Due to Inappropriate Minimum Wage Rate Determinations,* 1970, p. 23.

[10] Armand J. Thieblot, Jr., *The Davis-Bacon Act,* Labor Relations and Public Policy Series, Report No. 10 (Philadelphia: University of Pennsylvania Press, 1975), p. 50.

[11] Ibid.

[12] General Accounting Office, *Davis-Bacon Act,* Chapter 4 and Appendixes V to XI.

Labor Department costs are, however, only a fraction of the direct government costs associated with the act. The individual agencies administering the construction contracts are in the first instance responsible for enforcement of the act and must inform the Labor Department when they need wage determinations. In addition, they are required to provide contractors with information about rate schedules and to keep track of contractor payments to make sure that the prevailing wages are paid. Other costs arise when, as in the case of the Department of Housing and Urban Development, an agency establishes its own wage-rate determination staff.[13]

The Administrative Burden of Wage Determinations on Business

Most of the paperwork costs associated with the Davis-Bacon Act are, however, not borne by government directly, but rather by the contractors performing government work. It should be stressed that these costs are incorporated into the bids that contractors submit for work covered by the act. Perhaps the most costly is the payroll-reporting requirement, which stipulates that the prime contractor submit a weekly report containing the "name, address, social security number, number of withholding exemptions, number of hours worked each day of the week, total straight time hours and overtime hours worked each week, rate of pay, gross earnings, FICA, withholding tax and other deductions, and net wages paid for the week."[14] Furthermore, a monthly Manpower Utilization Report Form requires that "for each trade—and within the trade for the journeymen, helpers, apprentices, and trainees—the total man-hours of employment on federal and non-federal projects (separately), the Negro employment, the Spanish-surnamed, et cetera, the percent minority man-hours of total man-hours, the total minority employees, and the total number of employees."[15] The Associated General Contractors of America estimates that the combined expense of these and several other requirements amounts to one-half of 1 percent of overall contract costs, or a total annual expense of $190 million.[16] Whether the reams of paper that are filled with these figures are ever looked at may be doubted. "We feel that in many cases, the reports are filed and not even reviewed," reports one contractor. "We have purposely made errors on reports to check this out, and they have never been brought to our attention."[17]

---

[13] Thieblot, *Davis-Bacon Act*, p. 79.

[14] Ibid., p. 82.

[15] Ibid.

[16] Ibid., p. 80.

[17] Ibid.

A recent GAO study notes that the Commission on Government Procurement has concluded that the weekly reporting records are not an effective enforcement tool; violations of the act have only rarely been uncovered by review and verification of payrolls. The commission's recommendation, which was not adopted by the Labor Department, was that the requirement be abolished.[18]

General Accounting Office Studies

Nine studies by the General Accounting Office have documented instances in which Davis-Bacon wage determinations have been unusually high. A few of these studies are summarized below.

Capehart Housing in Quantico, Virginia. In March 1960 the Navy Department requested a specific determination for the Capehart housing project at the Marine Corps School in Quantico, Virginia, a community about thirty-five miles south of Washington, D.C. Its request noted that an earlier Labor Department determination contained wage rates very much in excess of a current area wage survey conducted by the officer in charge of this construction project. Table 2 compares these two sets of wage rates. It indicates that the Davis-Bacon determinations ran anywhere from 28 to 100 percent higher than the estimated "average" wages for the designated crafts in the area wage survey. On the basis of this information, the Labor Department issued a new determination with lower wage rates. Within a month, however, in response to union protests, the Labor Department reinstated the *original* wage rates. The Navy protested, but a hearing examiner decided in favor of the union rates, and these became the final determination. In its review of this case, GAO concluded:

- The Labor Department's determination did *not* represent prevailing wages.
- The inaccurate rates determined for this project raised wage costs by $1.1 million or about 15 percent of the total contract cost.[19]

Professor D. N. Gujarati notes that subsequent to the Quantico decision, three additional determinations for projects in the area carried local rates that were lower than the union rates.[20] While it is

---

[18] General Accounting Office, *Davis-Bacon Act*, pp. 80-81.

[19] U.S. General Accounting Office, *Review of Wage Rate Determinations for Construction of Capehart Housing at the Marine Corps School, Quantico, Virginia*, 1962.

[20] D. N. Gujarati, "The Economics of the Davis-Bacon Act," *Journal of Business*, vol. 40 (July 1967), pp. 303-16.

TABLE 2
Quantico Project Wage Data

Craft	Davis-Bacon Wage[a]	Area Survey Wage	Percentage by Which Davis-Bacon Exceeds Mid-Point of Area Survey Wages
Laborer	$2.42	$1.00–2.40	43
Carpenter	3.67	2.00–3.50	33
Cement mason	3.87	1.75–3.00	63
Bricklayer	4.15	2.75–3.75	28
Plumber	4.16	2.00–3.00	66
Electrician	4.45	2.00–3.50	62
Plasterer	4.10	1.60–3.00	78
Painter	3.84	1.50–2.35	100

[a] Rates are union rates for commercial construction in metropolitan Washington, D.C.

Sources: D. N. Gujarati, "The Economics of the Davis-Bacon Act," *Journal of Business*, vol. 40 (July 1967), Table 6, p. 313; and U.S. General Accounting Office, *Review of Wage Rate Determinations for Construction of Capehart Housing at the Marine Corps School, Quantico, Virginia*, 1962.

comforting to know that this downward adjustment was made for later projects, the adjustment provides further evidence that the Quantico decision was much too high. It is particularly alarming that the Labor Department insisted on union rates that had been imported from another area when it had unambiguous evidence that such rates were seriously in error.

Federally Financed Construction in New England. The General Accounting Office examined Davis-Bacon wage determinations for federally financed construction in New England in 1962. In his report to the Congress, the comptroller general stated:

> Our review of the determinations by the Department of Labor of minimum wage rates to be paid to mechanics and laborers employed on construction of federally financed building projects in selected New England areas disclosed that many of the rates were improperly established at the higher rates negotiated by labor organizations and building contractors rather than at the lower rates prevailing on private construction in the project areas. Also, wage rates determined for certain crafts in connection with a federally-assisted low-rent housing project in Massachusetts were on a level with the negotiated rates normally paid on

commercial-type building construction rather than equal to the lower rates paid on similar private housing construction in the locality. *Our review showed that these unrealistic determinations were based on inadequate information obtained by the Department on wage rates in these areas, and we believe that the Department has not complied with either its own regulations or the intent of the Davis-Bacon Act that wage determinations be based on the wage rates prevailing for similar construction in the locality.*[21]

The GAO report presented several interesting findings about Davis-Bacon determinations in New England:

1. Wage determinations for power equipment operators on federally financed projects throughout Maine were found to be higher than those prevailing in Maine. The Davis-Bacon rates corresponded to union-negotiated rates in Boston.

2. GAO noted several cases in which regular employees of non-union contractors worked at (or approximately at) the same time on private and federal projects and were paid higher rates on the federal projects. Comparative wages provided in the GAO report showed that employees working concurrently on the two kinds of projects earned wages on federal projects that were from 68 to 221 percent higher than their wages on private projects.

3. GAO found that the Department of Labor included previous Davis-Bacon rates in the information it used to determine prevailing wages on new contracts, thereby carrying any earlier errors forward. In the words of the GAO report:

> The [Labor] Department's survey disclosed that the average hourly rate for laborers, while working only on private construction in 1963, was $1.92 or 33 cents an hour lower. The 1962 wage decisions showed that the minimum rate for truck drivers was the negotiated rate of $2.15, but the Department's survey disclosed that the prevailing rate for truck drivers was $1.50 an hour . . . or 65 cents an hour lower than the negotiated rate. The difference in interpretation of the Department's recent survey stems from the fact that we have excluded from the survey data the wage rates paid on federally financed projects which were subject to prior wage decision of the Department employing the negotiated rate.[22]

---

[21] U.S. General Accounting Office, *Wage Rates for Federally Financed Building Construction Improperly Determined in Excess of the Prevailing Rates for Similar Work in New England Areas*, 1965. Emphasis added.

[22] Ibid., p. 15.

TABLE 3
New England Study Wage Data

Craft	Department of Labor Determination of Wage	GAO Private Housing Survey Wage	Difference
Mason	$4.12	$3.81	$0.31
Carpenter	3.85	3.04	0.81
Ironworker	4.26	2.51	1.75
Lather	3.90	2.75	1.15
Painter	3.30	2.28	1.02
Plumber	4.20	3.14	1.06
Plasterer	4.12	3.50	0.62
Laborer	2.90	2.23	0.67
Steamfitter	4.20	3.00	1.20
Soft-floor layer	3.85	3.08	0.77
Tile setter	4.05	2.58	1.47
Truck driver	2.80	2.40	0.40

SOURCE: U.S. General Accounting Office, *Wage Rates for Federally Financed Building Construction Improperly Determined in Excess of the Prevailing Rates for Similar Work in New England Areas,* 1965, p. 19. Wage rates are reported to the lowest cent.

4. The GAO report noted that ". . . as has been shown in this report and in associated reports to the Congress, it has been the practice of the Department to determine the higher negotiated rates paid on commercial type building construction as the minimum rates for federally financed housing construction instead of the lower wage rates prevailing for similar private housing construction in the project areas."[23] To estimate the difference attributable to this application of incorrect rates, the General Accounting Office surveyed construction costs of twenty-nine apartments in Middlesex, Suffolk, and Norfolk counties, Massachusetts, that were comparable to a low-rent housing project in Middlesex that carried a Davis-Bacon determination. The GAO did not choose the lowest possible rates, but rather applied the Labor Department's determination rule to the survey data. The results are shown in Table 3. On the average, over all the reported crafts, the Davis-Bacon determination was 33 percent greater than the GAO survey wage. It should be emphasized that the GAO figures are "prevailing" wages and are quite likely to be above the minimum wage in each craft.

[23] Ibid., p. 21.

21

Further GAO Studies. The findings of the Quantico and the New England studies were essentially repeated in 1968 and 1970 GAO studies.[24] These studies made some other relevant points. First, GAO found that, because of the high rates determined by the Labor Department for Davis-Bacon construction, open-shop, private housing contractors were sometimes reluctant to bid on such contracts. To do so

- would disrupt a company's labor force because workers on government jobs would be paid greater hourly rates than those on private jobs, and
- would create hardship and morale problems when workers' wage rates decreased after the government job was completed and they returned to work on private construction jobs.

This reaction of nonunion contractors to the excessive Davis-Bacon rates has two undesirable consequences. It limits the competition for government contracts, thereby raising the cost of these contracts. In addition, it suggests that the Davis-Bacon contracts tend to segregate the labor market to the disadvantage of nonunion workers.

Second, GAO found that the wage-information file of the Department of Labor was inadequate to determine appropriate wage rates. GAO also found that the department had conducted wage surveys in 1957 and in 1961 showing that nonnegotiated wage rates prevailed on privately constructed single-family homes in the Washington metropolitan area. The report goes on to state:

> Nevertheless, most of the current wage data in the Department's files at the time of our review consisted of data from negotiated wage agreements submitted by local labor organizations. We did not find in the files adequate current data showing the specific construction projects on which the negotiated wage rates prevailed, the specific construction projects on which nonnegotiated rates prevailed, or the number of workers being paid negotiated and nonnegotiated wage rates.[25]

Third, GAO noted that the department's determinations displayed a significant inconsistency. The department determined *different* classifications and minimum rates for similar low-rent public housing projects in the District of Columbia and in the nearby city of Alexandria, Virginia. The District of Columbia project was classified as

---

[24] General Accounting Office, *Need for More Realistic Minimum Wage Rate Determinations;* and General Accounting Office, *Construction Costs Increased.*
[25] General Accounting Office, *Need for More Realistic Minimum Wage Rate Determinations,* pp. 22-23.

commercial construction, whereas the department classified the similar project in Alexandria as residential construction.

In 1971 the General Accounting Office issued a summary report, which outlined the findings in seven earlier reports.[26] On the basis of its investigation of twenty-nine selected projects, GAO estimated that inappropriate wage determinations caused construction costs on these projects to be increased between 5 and 15 percent. Inappropriate determinations resulted because (1) the wage rates of one classification of worker were applied to another; (2) wage rates were used from a different area; (3) no distinction was made among workers in the same classification working on different types of projects; and (4) the wage determinations were based on previous determinations or on collective bargaining agreements without verification of whether such rates were representative of local wage rates.

As considerable discretion is possible in administering the Davis-Bacon Act, the report suggested that the secretary of labor adopt the following reforms:

> Formulate explicit guidelines and criteria covering the principal elements of an adequate wage determination. . . .
> Implement improved procedures for collecting needed data on basic wages and fringe benefits. To supplement its own efforts, the Department should establish with the principal Federal agencies financing construction contracts a formalized and continuing working relationship for the exchange of pertinent wage information.[27]

The report also recommended that helper and trainee classifications be included in the DOL wage determinations "where appropriate and in accordance with labor practices" and that Congress raise the minimum cost to which the act applies from $2,000 to an amount between $25,000 and $100,000 to ease the administrative burden on the department.

GAO Calls for Repeal

In 1979 the General Accounting Office released a new report on the Davis-Bacon Act that examined the administration of the act since it had issued its recommendations in 1971.[28] In an examination of

---

[26] U.S. General Accounting Office, *Need for Improved Administration of the Davis-Bacon Act Noted Over a Decade of General Accounting Office Reviews*, July 1971.

[27] Ibid., p. 3.

[28] General Accounting Office, *Davis-Bacon Act*.

seventy-three randomly selected Department of Labor determinations, GAO found that most of the undesirable practices cited in the earlier studies were still prevalent. Nearly one-half of the seventy-three determinations "were not supported by surveys of wages paid on similar construction projects in the locality. Labor relied on wage rates and corresponding worker classifications and work practices established in union-negotiated collective bargaining agreements to set wage rates in the locality of the construction."[29] Upon closer investigation of the 530 wage determinations in effect in October 1976, it was found that no survey was conducted for 302. In each case where no survey was made, the determination was based on union rates. Verification that the rates were in fact paid was sporadic, and "Labor did not determine how many workers were paid the rates in the locality or the extent of nonunion wages paid to workers engaged on similar work in the area."[30]

Other practices cited by GAO were the use of inaccurate data in surveys, arbitrary revision of data, the inappropriate extension of wage determinations across counties, the use of wage data from projects not similar to the one for which the determination was issued, and the use of previous determinations in establishing new ones. GAO's report concluded that the Davis-Bacon Act has not been and may never be properly administered, that the explicit protection of the wages of construction workers is now unnecessary because economic and legal conditions have changed, and that the act results in extra construction costs of several hundred million dollars annually. On the basis of these conclusions, GAO recommended that the act be repealed.

Alteration of Data Used for Surveys. According to the GAO report, the Department of Labor does undertake surveys in some instances, but an investigation of how those surveys are conducted uncovered indifferent and haphazard compliance with both the spirit and the letter of the act and with related administrative rules. In many cases, for example, changes were made in the data for no apparent reason. In other instances, changes were made that were of a more systematic character.

> [I]n some cases the Labor staff (1) added classifications at union-negotiated rates on which no data were received in the survey, (2) adjusted a rate, after union protest on a multi-county survey, and issued rates from combined counties on

---

29 Ibid., p. 40.
30 Ibid., p. 43.

all other classifications, (3) generally deleted the lowest rates, and (4) contrary to Labor's regulations, deleted and did not use data obtained in the survey on a piece rate basis.[31]

Such procedures were followed in the case of determinations for a residential housing project in Stanislaus County, California (project determination 76-CA-33). It was found that the wage specialist eliminated most of the lower rates obtained from the survey. In calculating the rate for carpenters, for example, rates for 113 workers between $2.50 and $4.50 were omitted. Including these rates would have resulted in a wage determination of $4.85. The actual determination was $6.54, or $1.69 higher than if the systematic exclusion of lower rates had not been followed.[32]

In the case of an Orange County, New York, project (project determination 76-NY-237), the GAO staff found a similar instance in which the rates were deliberately biased upward. An attempt was made by DOL to gather data on twelve classifications, and all but one rate received was lower than the union rates. Eleven classifications on which no data were obtained were added by the DOL headquarters staff, and the union rates were issued as the prevailing rates for all twenty-three classifications.[33]

Use of Data from Dissimilar Private Construction Projects. It was also noted that wage rates were frequently used from projects that bore scant resemblance to the project for which the determination was being made. In the case of a U.S. Postal Service project in Cumberland County, North Carolina (project determination 76-NC-29), which entailed overhauling an air conditioning unit, the Labor Department used figures from fifty-three projects. These ranged from the installation of a sprinkler system in a men's formal wear shop, to alterations and additions to a bus garage, to the construction of enlisted men's barracks. The dissimilarity of these projects can be shown by comparing the wage rates of workers of the same classification. Carpenters working on the bus garage received $3.75 an hour, those on a synthetic fiber plant $6.05. For electricians, the wages were $4.75 and $6.50; for laborers, $2.75 and $3.25.[34]

Use of Wage Rates Paid on Previous Federal Projects. Although the intent of the act is to ensure that construction workers employed on

---

[31] Ibid., p. 48.
[32] Ibid., Appendix VI, p. 149.
[33] Ibid., Appendix VI, p. 141.
[34] Ibid., Appendix VIII, p. 159.

TABLE 4

EFFECT OF DELETING PREVIOUS FEDERAL WAGE-RATE DETERMINATIONS
ON NEW PREVAILING-WAGE DETERMINATIONS

Project and Classification	Rate Issued by DOL	GAO-Computed Rate without Federal Projects	Percentage Difference (Higher)
Project determination 76-TN-88			
Dickson County, Tennessee			
Carpenter	$7.91	$6.00	31.8
Electrician	5.83	4.95	17.8
Laborer	4.65	3.73	24.7
Mason tender	4.80	5.00	(4.0)
Sheetmetal worker	8.37	9.62	(13.0)
Tilesetter	5.50	5.09	8.1
Bulldozer operator	7.30	4.93	48.1
Project determination 76-LA-122			
Rapides Parish, Louisiana			
Cement worker	5.00	5.70	(12.3)
Laborer	3.54	3.40	4.1
Roofer	5.23	5.40	(3.2)
Sheetmetal worker	6.67	7.07	(5.7)
Forklift operator	5.00	3.75	33.3

SOURCE: U.S. General Accounting Office, *The Davis-Bacon Act Should Be Repealed*, 1979, Appendix VII, pp. 154-55.

federal construction projects earn the wage prevailing for private construction at the time of each project, the Department of Labor has often used previously determined rates to come up with the rates for a new project. Table 4 shows what the effect of deleting the previous determinations would have been in two cases. Note that in five out of twelve occupations the determinations made without the previous rates were below the Labor Department's rates by at least 10 percent, and in three cases the Labor Department estimate was more than 30 percent higher. The practice of using previous determinations not only runs counter to the intent of the act, it also perpetuates errors made in previous determinations.

Use of Wages from Noncontiguous Counties. Of the seventy-three Department of Labor determinations examined by the General Accounting Office, fifty-six were complete enough to reveal the source of the rates issued. Nearly one-third of these determinations used rates from counties other than the one in which the project was located. In Tennessee, for example, wage determinations for projects in Dickson County (population 26,000) and in Monroe County (population 73,000) were based on the rates in noncontiguous Davidson County (population 447,000). In the case of Dickson County determinations, a survey was conducted three months after the determination was made. It was found that for fourteen comparable crafts, seven were lower than in the original determination, three were higher, and four were the same. In the case of the Montgomery County determination, a survey had been undertaken before the determination was made, but the headquarters staff instructed the regional staff to ignore it and to use the Davidson rates instead.[35]

Use of 30 Percent Rule. Typically, union-negotiated wages apply to all union workers of a classification, even though they may be working for different contractors. Open-shop employees, on the other hand, often receive wages that differ from contractor to contractor and from worker to worker, even within the same classification. These differences may be small, but the important point is that if they differ by as much as one cent, the effect will be to diminish the likelihood that an open-shop rate will be used to determine the prevailing wage rate. An example provided by GAO in its report illustrates this point. In a determination of wage rates for painters in Carson City, Nevada, the data available showed that eight painters received wages between $6.25 and $12.40 per hour. Three, or 37.5 percent, were paid the $12.40 rate; the others received from $6.25 to $9.00. According to the 30 percent rule, however, the prevailing wage must be the higher, union-negotiated wage.[36]

The report observed that "[i]n areas where unions have organized at least 30 percent of the construction workers, their wage scales have an excellent chance of becoming the prevailing rate even though 70 percent of the rates paid to other workers may vary by small amounts."[37] Moreover, these rates are, as we saw, perpetuated because the Department of Labor uses the figures from previous determinations in arriving at estimates of new prevailing rates. Consequently, if the proportion of union membership declines below 30 percent, their rates may nevertheless be held to prevail.

---

[35] Ibid., Appendix IX, pp. 163-65.
[36] Ibid., p. 52.
[37] Ibid.

TABLE 5

Union-Negotiated and Nonunion Rates Issued by the Department of Labor Compared with GAO Survey Rates

Region	Total Number of Wage Rates Compared	DOL Rates		GAO Survey Rates	
		Union-negotiated	Non-union	Union-negotiated	Non-union
New York	34	33	1	20	14
	(12)	(97)	(3)	(59)	(41)
Atlanta	75	16	59	3	72
	(27)	(21)	(79)	(4)	(96)
Chicago	46	35	11	18	28
	(17)	(76)	(24)	(39)	(61)
Dallas	43	34	9	14	29
	(16)	(79)	(21)	(33)	(67)
San Francisco	79	65	14	61	18
	(28)	(82)	(18)	(77)	(23)
Total	277	183	94	116	161
	(100)	(66)	(34)	(42)	(58)

Note: Figures in parentheses are percentages.
Source: U.S. General Accounting Office, *The Davis-Bacon Act Should Be Repealed*, 1979, p. 71.

Disproportionate Representation of Union Wage Data. Although Labor Department determinations seem designed to bias the determination procedure so that union rates come to be the "prevailing rate," it was found that, even according to these rules, Labor made determinations based on union rates in disproportionately large numbers of cases. GAO found that union rates prevailed in only 42 percent of the 277 worker classifications, but Labor issued union rates for 66 percent. As Table 5 shows, this bias held for determinations made in all regions.

Labor Department personnel, on the other hand, estimate that 40 to 45 percent of determinations are based on union wages.[38] They do not, however, have an estimate of the proportion of workers covered by determinations carrying union wages. Whatever the true figure for the fraction of determinations based on union rates, the fraction of workers covered by those rates is likely to be higher. Area determinations are typically made for metropolitan areas, and it is

---

[38] Library of Congress, Congressional Research Service, *Davis-Bacon Act*, p. 17.

there that unionization is highest. A single determination there would apply to as much work as is covered by several wage-rate determinations in less unionized areas.

Professor Gujarati's Study

As can readily be seen from the above sampling of the comptroller general's studies, many specific cases have been identified in which the Labor Department's Davis-Bacon wage-rate determinations were seriously in error on a number of counts. In some cases, the General Accounting Office's review focused on determinations that were known to be in error; in others, such as the most recent one, the wage determinations were picked randomly. As we saw, there has been a tendency on the part of the Labor Department to use local union rates as the prevailing rate or to import union rates from noncontiguous counties when most workers in an area are open-shop employees. This tendency was examined in considerable detail in 1965 by Professor D. N. Gujarati in his doctoral dissertation at the University of Chicago.[39] His study covered 300 counties from the fifty states, the District of Columbia, and Puerto Rico. In order to obtain more precise information on Labor Department determinations in cases where unionization was low, the counties were distributed among areas in inverse proportion to the extent of unionization in these areas.

Professor Gujarati's work sheds light on the following questions: (1) What is the locality that is in fact used for the purpose of making the wage determinations? (2) What proportion of determinations carry union wage rates? (3) What kinds of data are used to make the determinations?

Professor Gujarati collected data on 372 wage determinations for nine crafts in the sample counties. His detailed breakdown of these determinations is provided in Table 6. This table provides several interesting findings. First, the fraction p^*, which is the weighted proportion of determinations carrying union wage rates, is close to one in most instances. This means that nearly all determinations carried union wage rates. Professor Gujarati found it very difficult to measure the actual extent of unionization by craft, except in the case of common labor. He estimates that about 59 percent of common laborers are unionized. Yet their Davis-Bacon wage determinations were based

---

[39] D. N. Gujarati, *The Economics of the Davis-Bacon Act*, doctoral dissertation, Graduate School of Business, University of Chicago, 1965. A *Journal of Business* article based on this dissertation has been cited above.

TABLE 6
Davis-Bacon Determinations by Craft and by Type of Wage Rate Prevailing

Craft and Type of Construction	Union Wage Rate				Survey Wage		Payment Evidence		Total[a]	p*	σ_p[b]
	Local	Contiguous counties	Non-contiguous counties	Statewide	Union	Nonunion	Union	Nonunion			
Bricklayer: Building	58 (30.6)	52 (27.5)	45 (23.8)	7 (3.6)	1 (1.3)	— —	18 (9.5)	8 (4.2)	189	.9674	.0142
									—	—	—
Heavy and highway	2 (6.1)	8 (24.2)	6 (18.2)	9 (27.3)	1 (3.0)	— —	3 (9.1)	4 (12.1)	33	.8981	.0265
									—	—	—
Carpenter: Building	69 (32.6)	55 (26.1)	35 (16.6)	7 (3.6)	1 (0.3)	3 (1.4)	16 (7.6)	25 (11.8)	211	.9299	.0175
									—	—	—
Heavy and highway	12 (10.0)	15 (12.6)	8 (7.5)	39 (32.7)	— —	3 (2.5)	9 (7.5)	32 (27.2)	119	.7558	.0390
									—	—	—
Plasterer: Building	50 (27.3)	63 (34.5)	37 (20.2)	7 (3.8)	3 (1.6)	— —	17 (9.3)	6 (3.3)	183	.9798	.0100
									—	—	—
Heavy and highway	1 (5.6)	6 (33.4)	5 (27.7)	5 (27.7)	— —	— —	1 (5.6)	— —	18	1.0000	.0000
									—	—	—

Electrician: Building	54 (26.0)	68 (32.7)	45 (21.7)	9 (4.3)	2 (0.9)	1 (0.6)	17 (8.4)	11 (5.4)	207	.9658	.0142
Heavy and highway	6 (11.8)	11 (21.5)	16 (31.5)	13 (25.5)	—	—	2 (3.8)	3 (5.9)	51	.9383	.0360
Painter: Building	60 (28.4)	57 (27.1)	37 (17.5)	10 (4.7)	2 (0.9)	1 (0.5)	10 (4.7)	33 (16.2)	210	.8901	.0221
Heavy and highway	8 (14.7)	15 (27.9)	10 (18.5)	11 (20.5)	—	—	2 (3.2)	8 (14.7)	54	.9059	.0450
Plumber: Building	54 (27.8)	58 (29.9)	39 (20.1)	11 (5.7)	3 (1.5)	—	17 (8.8)	12 (6.2)	194	.9545	.0150
Heavy and highway	4	10	6	6	—	—	6	1	33	.9696	.0140
Power equipment operator: Building	53 (27.9)	51 (26.9)	38 (20.0)	28 (14.5)	1 (0.6)	—	13 (6.8)	6 (3.3)	190	.9769	.0110
Heavy and highway	11	9	9	46	1	1	11	25	113	.7461	.0400

(Table continued on next page.)

TABLE 6 (continued)

Craft and Type of Construction	Union Wage Rate				Survey Wage		Payment Evidence		Total[a]	p*	σ_p[b]
	Local	Contiguous counties	Non-contiguous counties	Statewide	Union	Nonunion	Union	Nonunion			
Common Laborer:											
Building	60	52	42	12	2	—	13	37	218	.8534	.0237
	(27.5)	(23.9)	(19.3)	(5.5)	(0.9)	—	(5.9)	(17.0)	—	—	—
Heavy and highway	15	14	10	39	—	1	3	48	129	.6722	.0396
	(11.6)	(10.9)	(7.8)	(29.5)	—	(0.8)	(2.3)	(37.1)	—	—	—
Cement Mason:											
Building	60	57	38	11	—	—	14	19	199	.9289	.0175
	(30.2)	(28.6)	(19.1)	(5.5)	—	—	(7.0)	(9.6)	—	—	—
Heavy and highway	11	14	12	21	1	—	7	20	86	.8549	.0380
	(12.8)	(16.3)	(13.9)	(24.4)	(1.2)	—	(8.1)	(23.3)	—	—	—

Notes: Figures in parentheses are percentages. Building construction includes commercial, residential, and building parts of missile construction. Heavy and highway construction includes interstate highways, dams, bridges, etc. Not all determinations required rates for all the nine crafts.

[a] The number of determinations for which wage rates were requested.

[b] The standard error of the estimate p*.

Source: D. N. Gujarati, "The Economics of the Davis-Bacon Act," *Journal of Business*, vol. 40 (July 1967), p. 306.

on union wages 85 percent of the time in the case of building construction, and 67 percent in the case of heavy and highway construction.

Second, perhaps the most telling evidence is the extent to which union wage rates are imported into a locality from noncontiguous counties or from statewide wage data. Professor Gujarati notes that Section I of the Davis-Bacon Act defines the area of construction as the "city, town, village, or other civil subdivision of the state in which the work is performed" and, further, that the legislative history of the act does not indicate that this definition was intended to be construed so loosely as to permit use of wages from noncontiguous counties. The intent of the act was to protect *local* wage rates, not to raise these local rates by basing determinations on rates from other, higher-wage-paying areas. Nonetheless, the survey data indicate that a substantial portion of the Davis-Bacon determinations use prevailing wages from noncontiguous counties. According to these data, from 25 to 38 percent of the building construction determinations were based on rates from noncontiguous counties, and 46 to 73 percent of the heavy and highway construction determinations. In some cases the Labor Department went beyond state boundaries for "prevailing"-wage data, as was noted in the GAO report on construction in New England.

A third noteworthy finding is that Department of Labor wage surveys were not generally used to determine prevailing wages. Indeed, in his sample of 372 wage determinations, Professor Gujarati found that surveys were made for only eight projects (or slightly more than 2 percent). On the other hand, unions were prompt to submit wage-rate data; this accounted, in part, for the strong preponderance of union wage determinations.

Further analysis of "noncontiguous county" determinations suggests the following additional findings. First, union wage-rate determinations based on rates from noncontiguous counties occur with greater frequency as the population of the county where the construction occurs decreases. This is illustrated in Figure 1, which is adapted from Professor Gujarati's data. He suggests that population may be a good proxy for the extent of unionization and, if this is so, it appears that union wages are imported into nonunion localities by the Davis-Bacon determinations.

Second, Professor Gujarati calculated for each craft the average distance in miles between the localities in which the noncontiguous wage data are applied and the counties from which the data are collected. These distances range from seventy-two to eighty-four miles,

FIGURE 1

Percentage of Determinations Based on Out-of-County Union Wage Rates, by County Population

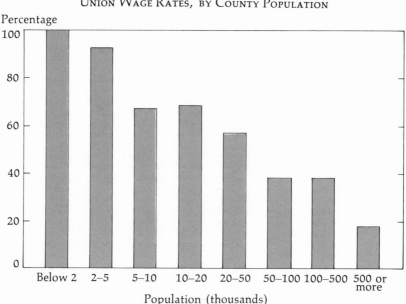

SOURCE: Adapted from D. N. Gujarati, "The Economics of the Davis-Bacon Act," *Journal of Business*, vol. 40 (July 1967), p. 309.

and Professor Gujarati noted that this suggests that the Labor Department goes beyond a reasonable commuting distance in search of "prevailing" wages.

University of Pennsylvania Study

In an extensive study of the Davis-Bacon Act, the Industrial Research Unit of the University of Pennsylvania's Wharton School noted the same administrative problems as did the various GAO reports and Professor Gujarati. Written by Professor Armand J. Thieblot, the study, in addition to reviewing previous work on the subject, took a detailed look at several cases not covered elsewhere. Also, it summarized the responses obtained from 1,402 construction contractors concerning their views on the administration of the Davis-Bacon Act.

Case Study. The tendency of the Department of Labor to provide wage determinations that are biased upward is illustrated by the controversy surrounding Metro Segment C-7 in Arlington County, Virginia.[40] In late 1971 the construction of the section of metropolitan Washington's subway system that would run through Arlington was opened for bids. Work on this sort of project is usually categorized as "heavy" construction and performed at lower rates than "building" construction. In the federal district there are few heavy construction projects, however. By tradition, such projects there are carried out under the higher building rates, although this is not the practice in northern Virginia. Nonetheless, the Department of Labor, in making its wage determinations for a project located in a separate civil subdivision, Arlington County, adopted the higher rates for the subway project.

A request for reconsideration was submitted by the Virginia Road Building Association, which argued that the proposed work was not like Washington building construction but, in fact, more closely resembled the construction of highway interchanges. They suggested that the complex interchange then under construction nearby for Interstate Highway I-95, known as the Shirley Highway "mixing bowl," provided a sample of wages more appropriate for a determination of the subway-project wages. Despite the support of a Virginia senator and of the federal highway administrator, the Department of Labor refused to reconsider its determination. A petition was then filed with the Wage Appeals Board, resulting in an order for a new determination. Samples of the original determinations, of the wage rates paid on the interchange project, and of the new determinations, which included a "building" and a "heavy" construction rate, are presented in Table 7. Note that the original determinations for most categories were about one-third higher than either the wages paid on the interchange or the new determinations for heavy construction.

Survey Results. The survey results tabulated by Professor Thieblot are of considerable interest. Of 10,000 questionnaires mailed to members of several contracting organizations, 1,402 usable responses were received. These represented a fair cross-section of contractors: about half were open shops; various types of construction were performed by responding firms; and open-shop firms performed 28.0 percent of their work in urban areas, while union firms performed 51.8 percent of their work there. [41] Among the questions asked were whether the Davis-Bacon wage determinations were greatly different from the contractors' own rates, and what the two rates were for different

---

[40] Thieblot, *Davis-Bacon Act*, pp. 109-20.
[41] Ibid., pp. 154-57.

TABLE 7
Wage Rates for Key Heavy-Construction Jobs under Different Rate Determinations

Selected Job Titles	Metro Rate #1[a]	I-95[b]	Arlington Highway[c]	Metro Rate #2 (Building)[d]	Metro Rate #2 (Heavy)[e]	% Difference, Metro Rate #2 (Heavy) to Metro Rate #1
Air compressor operator	6.07	3.12	3.87	7.16	3.00	50.6
Backhoe operator	6.65	3.37	5.33	7.74	4.50	32.3
Bricklayer	8.90	5.65	5.00	8.90	4.00	55.1
Bulldozer operator	5.85	3.22	4.55	7.14	4.33	26.0
Carpenter	7.37	4.90	5.17	7.37	5.06	31.3
Cement mason	7.24	5.70	4.83	7.24	6.80	6.1
Common laborer	5.72	2.87	3.17	5.72	3.00	47.6
Iron worker (reinforcing)	7.12	4.45	4.50	7.48	4.45	37.5
Loader operator (over 2 yards)	5.95	3.22	5.20	7.59	4.75	20.2
Motor grader operator (fine)	5.95	3.37	4.87	6.94	4.90	17.6
Pipelayer	5.92	3.25	3.97	5.87	4.35	26.5
Powderman	6.37	3.25	—	6.90	—	—
Truck driver (dump)	4.07	2.87	3.88	4.47	3.25	20.1
Truck driver (multi-axle)	4.17	2.97	3.25	4.57	4.00	4.1
Average, 14 rates (mean)	6.24	3.73	4.43	6.79	4.34	30.4

[a] Decision AM-5,434, October 8, 1971.

[b] "Mixing bowl" determination, reported by Arlington County Manager.

[c] Arlington County highway contracts (average of five) actually being paid, November 26, 1971, as reported by Arlington County Manager.

[d] Decision AM-9208, December 13, 1971, building rates.

[e] Decision AM-9208, December 13, 1971, heavy rates.

SOURCE: Armand J. Thieblot, Jr., *The Davis-Bacon Act*, Labor Relations and Public Policy Series, Report No. 10 (Philadelphia: University of Pennsylvania Press, 1975), Table 15, pp. 116-17.

categories of workers. The results are presented in Table 8. Note that Department of Labor determinations were perceived to be substantially different from their own rates by open-shop contractors. Union firms, on the other hand, claimed no substantial difference in nearly 90 percent of the responses. A comparison of rate examples submitted by *all* categories of contractors reveals that the Davis-Bacon rates were above the contractors' own rates by roughly 30 to 40 percent. This implies that, for open-shop contractors, the difference was typically greater still.

Summary

Our review of the administration of the Davis-Bacon Act determinations suggests that these determinations are inappropriately (and often illegally) high in a substantial number of cases and that these deter-

---

TABLE 8

RESPONSES TO UNIVERSITY OF PENNSYLVANIA DAVIS-BACON
SURVEY OF 1,402 CONTRACTORS, SUMMER 1974

I. Respondent answers (in percent) to the question: "Were the wage-rate determinations (for Davis-Bacon) greatly different in either rate or benefits from your own on private work?"

	Yes	No
Union firms	10.8	89.2
Open shops	78.0	22.0
Doublebreasted	54.1	45.9

II. Rate comparisons based on the average of rate examples submitted by all categories of contractors.

	Own Rate	Davis-Bacon Rate	Percent Increase
Carpenters	$5.51	$7.30	32
Cement masons	5.30	6.95	31
Laborers	3.72	5.23	41
Plumber/pipefitter	5.87	7.78	33
Other trades	5.48	7.85	43
Average increase			36

III. Davis-Bacon labor as percent of total job costs: 31.1 percent.

SOURCE: Thieblot, *Davis-Bacon Act*, Table 20, p. 158.

minations do not conform to the intent of the act. Whether this situation is an unfortunate consequence of the huge burden imposed on the small staff responsible for making wage determinations or whether it arises for other reasons is immaterial as far as the consequences are concerned. Whatever the cause, Davis-Bacon determinations have tended to raise wages in the construction industry, and have spread high wages to various geographical localities irrespective of the wage rates actually prevailing in those localities. To the extent that faulty wage determinations discourage or make impossible participation of nonunionized construction firms in federal construction, the administration of the act has also strengthened the position of unionized construction labor.

Shortcomings in the determination of Davis-Bacon wage rates have led many investigators, including the comptroller general, to recommend improvements in the wage determination procedure. There is no evidence, however, despite several assurances to the contrary by Labor Department officials, that the determination procedure can ever be significantly improved. The poor record of determinations under the act is, in fact, strong evidence to the contrary and has led the General Accounting Office, after nine studies of the administration of the act, to conclude that it should be repealed.

Leaving the matter there, however, ignores an important question: Is such a prevailing-wage restriction, even if properly administered, a desirable policy? It seems likely that the act would have undesirable consequences even if the determinations were made in strict accordance with the secretary of labor's directive on wage-determination procedures. This issue and the economic costs of the act will be taken up in the next chapter.

4

The Effect of the Davis-Bacon Act
on the Cost of Construction Projects

Although it is clear that the Davis-Bacon Act has not been properly administered, there are good grounds for doubting whether a prevailing-wage law of any sort is required in construction or, for that matter, in any other industry. The arguments advanced in support of the act—that contractors engaged in competitive bidding for government projects have an incentive to cut wages, and that the act offsets the destabilizing forces in a fundamentally volatile industry—for the most part ignore the way wages are set in the economy.

An understanding of how labor markets work and how wages are determined is also a key ingredient in the measurement of social costs arising from the act. In its economic aspects, an effective union is a monopoly. A union's monopoly power is achieved by its restriction of entry into the trade and by its ability to withhold labor (its own and that of potential strikebreakers) and thereby negotiate wages that are higher than those that would prevail in a competitive market. As we shall see, the Davis-Bacon Act is the means by which substantial amounts of construction activity are transferred from the nonunion to the union sector, in effect increasing the demand that the monopolist faces. The exercise of monopoly power results in the imposition of losses on the rest of society, and increasing the scope of that power results in greater losses. The costs that are of interest in the case of the Davis-Bacon Act are the following: (1) inflated construction costs that represent a transfer to workers lucky enough to be paid wages greater than they would earn if they were offering their services on the open market, as most workers do; (2) costs to the contractors of complying with the regulations; (3) administrative costs to government agencies including, but not confined to, determinations conducted by the Department of Labor; and (4) the benefit that the public forgoes when government agencies or others affected by Davis-Bacon wage determinations decide not to undertake a project because those determinations result in increased costs.

The Basis for Wage Differentials

Numerous wage differentials can be found in the United States among workers of different industries, occupations, races, sexes, skills, educational attainments, union affiliations, geographic locations, and so on. The reasons for these differentials are almost as varied as the differentials themselves. In some cases, the wage differential reflects differences in productivity. In other instances, the differential is countered by differentials in nonpecuniary aspects of the job. High-paying jobs may in some cases be more hazardous or more demanding. Low-paying jobs may provide nonmonetary rewards such as a pleasant climate, a nicer work environment, greater employment security, or compensation in the form of training. Differences in wages can also arise from changes in market structures. For example, unions may be able to raise relative wages by limiting entry of workers into the craft or trade, by superior bargaining power, and by other means.[1]

These kinds of differentials may exist in a static equilibrium, but wage differentials also play a major role in the dynamics of a changing economy. Consider the case of two geographically distinct markets. Suppose that demand for housing in one of these markets increases relative to demand in the other market. The initial effect of this change in relative demand will be to raise construction wages in the high-demand market relative to wages in the low-demand market. If this wage differential is large enough, workers in the low-demand market will be encouraged to offer their services in the high-demand market. This supply response has two desirable effects. First, it serves to equilibrate wages in the two markets by raising wages in the low-demand market and by lowering wages in the high-demand market. This spreads the wage benefits of increased demand to all workers. Second, it facilitates the resource flow for which consumers have shown a preference by their change in demand—relatively more housing is built in the high-demand market and relatively less in the low-demand market.

This example illustrates the central role that wage and other price differentials play in determining resource flows in a market economy.

---

[1] Professor H. G. Lewis has provided a careful and scholarly analysis of the effect of unions on wages in *Unionism and Relative Wages in the United States* (Chicago: University of Chicago Press, 1963).

If wages are not permitted to respond to changing market conditions, many undesirable consequences can result. Suppose wages are frozen by law at the high relative level that obtains immediately following the increase in demand in the above example. Workers will be encouraged to refuse lower-paying jobs while attempting to search for work in the high-wage market. Since wages in this market are not allowed to drop, there will not be enough demand to absorb these additional workers. One result may be that frictional unemployment increases as workers spend more time searching for higher-paying job opportunities.[2] In addition, the flow of resources from the low-demand to the high-demand market is thwarted by the wage freeze. It can be demonstrated that this results in a welfare loss to society.

Another consequence of such a frozen wage differential is to create an artificial inequity in wages. As noted in the example, the shift of workers to the high-wage area lowers wages there and raises wages in the low-wage area. By freezing wages in the high-demand area, more workers are forced into the low-demand market, thereby reducing their wage rate relative to what it would be in an unconstrained market. This inequity runs directly counter to the claims of fairness that proponents of the Davis-Bacon Act make for it. In an unconstrained market, increases in demand tend to spread across the economy to the benefit of all workers. Constraints on wage changes concentrate the gains of additional demand on some workers at the expense of lower wages for others.

Another factor that needs to be taken into account is that there are considerable and *persistent* differences in wages paid at different locations. It has long been recognized, for example, that there are differences between the wages paid in the North and those paid in the South to workers with equal skills. These differences continue to exist despite considerable migration, both to the North in the early part of this century and, more recently, to the South and West. Similarly, though this has not been as widely recognized, there are often considerable differences in pay for similar jobs in the same state or county. Typically, the wages paid to workers in large cities are higher to compensate for the generally higher cost of living there. For workers who live outside the city, the higher wages reflect the cost of commuting to work. Often there are even differences in the same city that arise from these factors. For example, a study of the Chicago labor market found that, for all seven categories of blue-collar workers

---

[2] This phenomenon is described by John J. McCall in "Economics of Information and Job Search," *Quarterly Journal of Economics*, vol. 84 (February 1970), pp. 113-26.

examined, wages were higher in the heavily industrialized southwest part of the city than elsewhere.[3]

These differences in wages, which may be substantial, represent differences in cost of living, not differences in how well off workers are in fact. This point is especially important in view of the extensively documented tendency of the Department of Labor to import wage rates, sometimes from adjacent counties and sometimes from noncontiguous counties 100 or more miles away.[4] Curiously, although administrative practices betray a cavalier attitude toward such distinctions, the framers of the law seem to have been aware of them. The emphasis in the legislation is on the *prevailing* wage of the "city, town, village, or other civil subdivision of the State in which the work is to be performed."

It should be noted that those writing the law seem also to have been aware of the other factors that contribute to workers' receiving different wages. The law not only provides for separate determinations for relatively small geographical areas, but, as we have seen, for separate determinations for the different categories of workers, and even for different categories of projects. If the feeling had been that construction wages are set arbitrarily and without regard to varying circumstances, these issues would not have been addressed. It is precisely this variety in economic circumstances, however, that makes the law difficult to administer effectively. The Davis-Bacon Act in effect charges the Department of Labor with the continuous monitoring of a welter of economic detail. Yet this monitoring is unnecessary, since those directly affected—such as the plumber, the backhoe operator, and the plasterer—have every incentive to keep abreast of market conditions in their own area and elsewhere and to offer their services where they stand to gain the most.

Construction Employment

Approximately one out of twenty nonagricultural workers is employed in the contract construction industry. This has been a fairly stable relationship since World War II; since 1960 the figure has remained between 4.5 and 5.3 percent.[5] One of the frequently observed features

---

[3] A. Rees and G. Shultz, *Workers and Wages in an Urban Labor Market* (Chicago: University of Chicago Press, 1970), p. 179.

[4] An instance in which the Department of Labor attempted to include wages from projects as far away as 225 miles is described in Armand J. Thieblot, Jr., *The Davis-Bacon Act*, Labor Relations and Public Policy Series, Report No. 10 (Philadelphia: University of Pennsylvania Press, 1975), pp. 121-26.

[5] U.S. Office of the President, *Employment and Training Report of the President*, 1977, Table C-1, p. 218.

TABLE 9

Unemployment Rates for Selected Industries
(percent)

Year	All Industries	Construction	Manufacturing	Transportation and Public Utilities
1957	4.3	10.9	5.1	3.3
1958	6.8	15.3	9.3	6.1
1959	5.5	13.4	6.1	4.4
1960	5.5	13.5	6.2	4.6
1961	6.7	15.7	7.8	5.3
1962	5.5	13.5	5.8	4.1
1963	5.7	13.3	5.7	4.2
1964	5.2	11.2	5.0	3.5
1965	4.5	10.1	4.0	2.9
1966	3.8	7.1	3.2	2.0
1967	3.8	6.6	3.6	2.3
1968	3.6	6.9	3.3	1.9
1969	3.5	6.0	3.3	2.2
1970	4.9	9.7	5.6	3.2
1971	5.9	10.4	6.8	3.8
1972	5.6	10.3	5.6	3.5
1973	4.9	8.8	4.3	3.0
1974	5.6	10.6	5.7	3.2
1975	8.5	18.1	10.9	5.6
1976	7.7	14.4	7.9	4.7
1977	7.0	12.7	6.7	4.7

Source: U.S. Office of the President, *Employment and Training Report of the President*, 1978, Table A-22, p. 216.

of the construction industry is the tendency for construction workers to experience rates of unemployment higher than those of workers with similar demographic characteristics and skill levels. Table 9 presents recent unemployment figures for workers in construction, manufacturing, and transportation and public utilities, as well as for the population as a whole. Construction unemployment is typically twice as high as manufacturing, running on average in excess of 10 percent for the 1970s. This sort of evidence has frequently been used to argue that repeal of Davis-Bacon, or even alteration of the procedures governing its administration, would impose further setbacks on workers already suffering substantial hardships. Yet the contention that construction workers are in a fundamentally unusual situation must be questioned. Their higher rates of unemployment have tended to persist despite the passage of considerable time. High unemployment rates have not discouraged young workers from entering the field, nor have they convinced workers already in construction to leave. If one looks only at the unemployment figures, the impression is that construction work is undertaken as a labor of love and at a considerable sacrifice to the individual worker.

Some other evidence, however, suggests why workers might be willing to endure high unemployment rates. In particular, the hourly wage earned by construction workers is higher than that received by nonagricultural workers generally and higher than either the wage in manufacturing or the wage in transportation and public utilities, as Table 10 shows. This difference is also persistent, with the premium on construction wages over manufacturing wages running as high as 50 percent.

To what are the higher wages and higher unemployment rates in construction due? One reason for the higher wages, but one that does not explain the full difference, may be the influence of labor unions. On average, construction workers have higher rates of unionization than workers in general. Another, more fundamental, reason is that employment in the construction industry undergoes considerable fluctuation. Some of this volatility is related to usual business-cycle factors. Industries that supply relatively more durable goods, such as industrial equipment and structures, are more greatly affected by swings in aggregate demand than are those supplying goods such as food and clothing. The principal reason for this, of course, is that while the purchase of durable goods, often requiring considerable expenditures, can be postponed, the purchase of other items, of which we buy a week's or a month's worth at a time, cannot. Contract construction, as it happens, is among the industries most affected by general business conditions.

That, however, is not the whole story. Construction is also unstable over the calendar year. In some regions, conditions make it difficult to work during the winter. Construction unemployment usually then goes up. This pattern is accentuated by the availability of unemployment compensation, which increases the incentives employers have to lay workers off during the part of the year when construction is difficult and to hire them back later. In housing construction, this seasonal pattern is reinforced by people's preference for moving in the summer (in part so that their children's school year will not be broken up). Since the typical one-family house can be constructed in a few months, and since it would be costly to build a

TABLE 10

HOURLY EARNINGS OF PRODUCTION OR OF NONSUPERVISORY WORKERS,
TOTAL PRIVATE NONAGRICULTURAL ECONOMY AND SELECTED INDUSTRIES

Year	Total Private Economy	Construction	Manufacturing	Transportation and Public Utilities
1957	$1.89	$2.71	$2.04	—
1958	1.95	2.82	2.10	—
1959	2.02	2.93	2.19	—
1960	2.09	3.07	2.26	—
1961	2.14	3.20	2.32	—
1962	2.22	3.31	2.39	—
1963	2.28	3.41	2.45	—
1964	2.36	3.55	2.53	$2.89
1965	2.46	3.70	2.61	3.03
1966	2.56	3.89	2.71	3.11
1967	2.68	4.11	2.82	3.23
1968	2.85	4.41	3.01	3.42
1969	3.04	4.79	3.19	3.62
1970	3.23	5.24	3.35	3.85
1971	3.45	5.69	3.57	4.21
1972	3.70	6.06	3.82	4.65
1973	3.94	6.41	4.09	5.02
1974	4.24	6.81	4.43	5.41
1975	4.53	7.31	4.83	5.88
1976	4.86	7.70	5.22	6.45
1977	5.24	8.09	5.67	6.99
1978	5.69	8.65	6.17	7.54

NOTE: Dashes signify that data were not available.
SOURCE: U.S. Bureau of Labor Statistics, *Employment and Earnings*, February 1979, Table C-1, p. 91.

house and leave it unoccupied for any length of time, construction of such housing tends to take place just before the first occupants move in.

The evidence on unemployment rates and wages in Tables 10 and 11 also suggests that the higher unemployment rates arising from the more volatile nature of construction activity are more than compensated for by higher wage rates. Although an unemployment rate refers to the fraction of a labor force not employed at a point in time, it can also be interpreted as the fraction of time a typical member of that labor force may expect to be unemployed. In 1977, for example,

TABLE 11

Construction and Manufacturing Wages Adjusted for Unemployment, Selected Years, 1960–1977

Year	Adjusted Construction Wage	Adjusted Manufacturing Wage	Percentage by Which Construction Wage Exceeded Manufacturing Wage
1960	$2.66	$2.12	25.4
1965	3.33	2.51	33.7
1970	4.73	3.16	49.7
1975	6.00	4.30	39.5
1977	7.06	5.29	33.5

Source: Derived from Tables 9 and 10. See text for explanation.

the average wage in construction was $8.09 and the average unemployment rate 12.7 percent. By multiplying these two figures, we arrive at the amount by which construction wages could be reduced and yet leave workers with the same yearly income if they worked 100 rather than only 87.3 percent of the time; that is, if there were no unemployment in construction. By this calculation we get a figure of $1.03 as the "unemployment premium," and $7.06 as the construction wage after adjustment for time spent out of work.

Table 11 extends these calculations over several years for construction and manufacturing. It turns out that, even after adjusting for higher rates of unemployment, the construction wage is still greater than the manufacturing wage. The difference has varied, however, as the last column of Table 11 shows. Twenty years ago construction work earned only about a 25 percent premium. This figure increased to nearly 50 percent by 1970; it has declined somewhat since. These figures are only a partial measure of the compensation construction workers receive because they do not include unemployment compensation and unreported outside income.

What is the effect of unionization on the construction-industry labor market? Overall, about 40 percent of construction workers belong to a labor union. This percentage varies considerably from region to region, with higher figures found in metropolitan areas.[6] The percentage also varies by the type of construction performed and by the

---

[6] Thieblot, *Davis-Bacon Act*, pp. 203-4.

size of the firm. Workers involved in residential construction have very low union-membership rates; those in such fields as commercial building construction have higher rates. The union wage, as we saw in Chapter 3, is typically 20 to 40 percent higher. It should also be noted that work carried out by union employees is, as a rule, conducted under restrictions that do not apply to nonunion workers. These determine the maximum number of machines a worker may operate in a day, the sort of work to be reserved for a given trade specialization, and the ability of a contractor to hire his workers through the union hiring hall or by other means. One restriction that is of particular importance in a discussion of the Davis-Bacon Act is the requirement that union journeymen have completed an apprenticeship program. This apprenticeship program must in most cases be approved by the U.S. Bureau of Apprenticeship and Training, in which the labor unions have a considerable voice. The effect is to limit the number of apprentices and, as a result, the number of union journeymen.

It is sometimes argued that the higher wages of union employees simply reflect their greater productivity. This must be questioned, however. A large part of the negotiated contract between unions and contractors does not concern remuneration, but focuses instead on work rules. These rules are universally considered by contractors to decrease productivity. From the contractor's standpoint, there is every incentive to attempt to squeeze two dollars' worth of extra effort from a worker to whom he is compelled to pay two extra dollars. (There is considerable flexibility in the pace at which workers can produce, and most workers seem willing to give up some income for a more leisurely pace.) The aim with negotiated work-place practices appears to be to keep both the money and the more leisurely pace. The claim of higher union-worker productivity must be questioned on other grounds as well. For instance, if union workers were more productive, they could obtain higher wages without union activity.[7]

The inability of organized labor to establish effectively union shops for all types of construction firms has the following implications. Some types of construction are carried out predominantly by unionized firms. As mentioned, these are the construction of large projects requiring capital-intensive techniques and construction conducted by large firms in urban areas. Other types are performed by firms that are disproportionately nonunion, in particular the construction of residential housing. Yet a third category is conducted

---

[7] For a discussion of productivity among labor-union members, see Albert Rees, *The Economics of Trade Unions* (Chicago: University of Chicago Press, 1962).

by both and, as it happens, probably in an inefficient manner. Although the costs of the two types of firms for such construction are the same, both are doing it at a cost higher than would be possible in the absence of unions. Unionized firms must pay higher wages, while nonunion firms operate on a scale that is too small or with less than optimal capital. They continue at that scale, however, because changes would lead to their being unionized. These distinctions are important for identifying the types of construction in which substantial cost savings are possible if Davis-Bacon requirements do not apply. At least in the short run, savings could be expected for those types of construction for which the private sector already hires nonunion contractors. Over a longer period, it is very likely that some types of construction, especially those in which a large share of the work is covered by the Davis-Bacon Act, will increasingly be undertaken by nonunion firms.

The Relationship between Wages and Construction Costs

As currently administered, the Davis-Bacon Act discourages nonunion contractors from bidding on projects covered by the act or by legislation with similar provisions. This is done by specifying a wage rate that is higher than what nonunion contractors habitually pay and by establishing worker classifications that are in almost one-to-one correspondence with those in union agreements. In analyzing the economic effect of the law on the level of wages in the construction industry, as well as on the cost of construction covered by the act, it is necessary to consider what the aims of labor unions might be. It seems reasonable to assume that, at least in the long run, unions want to maintain the spread between their members' wages and the wages of those in the nonunionized sector. The obvious way to maintain this spread is to allow membership to fluctuate when the demand for union labor changes, as it might if the demand for the type of construction dominated by unions shifts or if changes are made in the Davis-Bacon Act. It is also necessary to have some idea of the response of the open-shop labor market. The most plausible long-run situation is that workers enter and leave fairly easily, that the supply of labor to open-shop contractors is elastic.

Data from studies conducted by the General Accounting Office show that inappropriate determinations run as much as 100 percent above the "true" prevailing wage. It should be pointed out, however, that so long as determinations are substantially above nonunion wages, and so long as the prescribed categories correspond closely to those in union wage contracts, the determination of prevailing wages *exactly* equal to union wages is unnecessary. Even if the determinations fall short of the union rates, it is likely that the act would result in work being carried out at those rates if open-shop firms are discouraged from bidding. We will, however, consider the wage determined by the Department of Labor to be the union wage for expository convenience, because of the bias inherent in the use of the 30 percent rule, and because the tendency of the Department of Labor to use union rates is, if not universal, at least widespread.

With these assumptions, we see that the effect of specifying that union wages be paid on a certain category of projects is to increase the amount of construction carried out under union rates and to decrease the amount of open-shop construction. The exact increase in hours worked in the union sector will depend on the fraction of work that nonunion contractors would otherwise successfully bid for and on the degree to which contractors can substitute machines for workers in their operations. In other words, the new average wage would be calculated by applying changed weights to the old wages. Union wages and open-shop wages are, by assumption, fixed. The extra cost is measured by the difference between union and nonunion wages times the amount of work (measured in construction-worker-hours) brought under union wages.

It is possible to gain a rough notion of these extra costs by looking at the size of the union wage premium and at the effect on construction costs of higher wages. Our discussion of Department of Labor wage determinations indicates that a conservative estimate for the union wage differential is 20 to 60 percent. Department of Labor estimates indicate that the wage premium for laborers was 45 to 75 percent in September 1973. For cement masons, plumbers, and electricians the premium was between 40 and 60 percent.[8] The fraction of construction costs going to labor is typically 30 percent, although this figure may be as low as 20 or as high as 40 percent for certain types of projects.[9] If there is no possibility of substituting other factors for labor, and if labor costs account for 30 percent of total costs, then a 30 percent increase in the construction wage will result in a 9 percent increase in total construction costs. If it is

---

[8] U.S. Bureau of Labor Statistics, *Industry Wage Survey: Contract Construction, September 1973*, Bulletin 1911, 1973, p. 5.

[9] Labor Department estimates assembled by Thieblot, *Davis-Bacon Act*, Table A-1, p. 185, indicate that labor costs account for the following percentages of total costs for selected categories of projects: single-family housing, 25.7; public housing, 39.2; industrial buildings, 25.0; commercial buildings, 28.0; hospitals, 32.6; public buildings, 32.0; highways, 25.2; and dams, 22.0.

possible to substitute other factors for labor, then the increase will be less. By making use of the concept of elasticity, we may conveniently express the range of outcomes under varying assumptions about the size of wage increases due to unions and the rise in construction costs due to increased wages. Table 12 indicates that, under conservative assumptions concerning the elasticity of substitution between labor and other factors and the share of cost going to labor, compelling contractors to pay wages at the union rate will result in an increase in construction costs of between 5 and 20 percent.

It is important to keep in mind that, except in the case where no substitution between labor and other factors is possible, the increase in construction costs represents not only a payment to labor but also a social loss. This social loss comes about because contractors are induced to use resources inefficiently when the price of labor is artificially high. In addition, some of the amount actually going to workers represents an extra element of the total social loss. This extra loss arises because workers use up resources in their attempts

TABLE 12

PERCENTAGE INCREASE IN CONSTRUCTION COSTS AS A FUNCTION OF THE
SIZE OF THE UNION WAGE PREMIUM

Union Wage Premium (percentage)	Elasticity = 0		Elasticity = 1.0	
	20% of costs to labor	40% of costs to labor	20% of costs to labor	40% of costs to labor
20	4.0	8.0	3.7	7.6
40	8.0	16.0	7.0	14.4
60	12.0	24.0	9.9	20.7

NOTE: Elasticity refers to the elasticity of substitution between labor and all other factors. The case when this elasticity (σ) equals zero is handled quite easily by noting that if c = unit costs, w = wage rate, and r = return to all other factors, then $c = a \cdot w + b \cdot r$ where a and b are parameters. For any percentage change in the wage ($\dot{w}$), the percentage change in unit costs is simply $\dot{w}$ times the share going to labor, $a \cdot w$. For $\sigma = 1$, we focus on the Cobb-Douglas unit-cost function $c = aw^{\alpha}r^{1-\alpha}$. Note that for infinitesimal changes in w, the percentage change in costs is also the share of the costs going to labor, α. This holds for infinitesimal changes in the input prices of any cost function. The results above are for discrete changes when $\sigma = 1$ and, although substantial, lie uniformly below the values for the case of $\sigma = 0$. The value of σ in the case of construction work is probably quite small, perhaps about one-half and certainly less than 1. The figures indicate that the change in unit costs is still substantial, even under fairly liberal assumptions about this elasticity.

to get union jobs—working at temporary positions while they wait to be accepted by the union or undergoing apprenticeships that are widely considered to be needlessly long and unproductive. Considerable resources are also spent by unions on lobbying, public relations, and in-house organizational activity. These efforts are primarily directed at maintaining the supracompetitive wages that members of construction unions enjoy. If we applied marginal analysis to these activities, as with any other economic activity, we might find that unions would be willing to spend ninety-nine cents to prevent the loss of one dollar. With several hundred million dollars at stake, expenditures to maintain and protect a union's position and organizational structure could conceivably amount to a substantial fraction of that amount. If, as we contend here, the union wage premium is largely unwarranted, then a substantial portion of the extra payments going to union members represents not a transfer but a loss.[10]

Now it may not be the case that the aim of unions is to keep their wage a certain level above that earned in the nonunionized sector of the economy. This seems particularly plausible over the short run, because it would be easier for unions to absorb short-run fluctuations in demand by varying their wages than by changing the number of union members.[11] The possibility that this may be the case in turn suggests that prevailing-wage legislation in general

---

[10] The issue may be more complicated than this, although the extra complications do not increase or decrease the total social costs and transfers caused by the simultaneous influence of unionization and the Davis-Bacon Act. As indicated, in certain categories of projects chiefly carried out by union contractors and others, both union and open-shop contractors compete. The winning bids on some government contracts will be those of union contractors, even in the absence of the act. Similarly, there may be a range of projects on which union bids are only slightly higher. Since the effect of the act is to award to open-shop firms work on this last category of projects and on those in which open-shop firms would otherwise have a large competitive edge, the savings from the repeal of the Davis-Bacon Act would be the sum of the differences between union and nonunion bids, and not the total decrease in government construction costs that would result if all workers were paid open-shop wages. In the long run, however, if repeal of the act lowers the degree of unionization, then extra savings would be realized.

[11] This also suggests that one of the features of the Davis-Bacon Act that unions find attractive is that it helps to smooth out the demand for union labor. Government construction tends to be less cyclically sensitive than private construction—indeed, a major aim of fiscal policy is to undertake projects with the intention of offsetting fluctuations in the private sector. If a sizable fraction, let us say one-third or one-half, of the employment of labor unions is covered by Davis-Bacon, the effect will be to reduce the volatility of union employment. This is accomplished, however, at the expense of increasing the volatility of employment in the nonunion sector.

TABLE 13

HYPOTHETICAL EXAMPLE OF THE EFFECT OF INELASTIC DEMAND

Wage (per man-hour)	Private Market Demand (man-hours)	Government Demand (man-hours)	Total Demand, Private and Government (man-hours)
$2.00	10,000	600	10,600
3.00	9,000	600	9,600
4.00	8,400	600	9,000
5.00	7,980	600	8,580
6.00	7,600	600	8,200

would tend to raise union wages. Although we have tended to emphasize the consequences of the faulty procedures through which Davis-Bacon determinations are made, it is reasonable to expect that the Davis-Bacon Act (and related prevailing-wage legislation) would tend to increase wages *even if local wages were accurately reflected* in the determination of prevailing wages. This is because the Davis-Bacon Act per se may alter the market structure and the nature of competition in the industry. This possibility has been pointed out and investigated by Ronald Ehrenberg, Marvin Kosters, and Michael Moskow.

The analytical basis for this argument is easy to demonstrate in a hypothetical numerical example. The Davis-Bacon Act and related laws tend to make government demand (and government-assisted demand) for construction projects relatively unresponsive (or inelastic) to wages. In other words, the act tends to decrease the government's bargaining power by disallowing the possibility of withholding contracts from high-wage bidders if these bidders can establish their wage as "prevailing." This tendency is augmented by the bias toward inappropriately high prevailing-wage determinations, but it would occur in any situation in which the government is prevented from searching out the lowest bidder. To see the effect of this inelastic demand on market wages, consider the following hypothetical example.

The first two columns in Table 13 show the demand for man-hours of construction work in the private market at various wage rates. Suppose there are 9,000 man-hours available. Then demand will equal supply, and the market will clear at a wage rate of $3.00 an hour. If the government enters this market with a demand for

600 man-hours of labor at any price (column 3), the total demand (government and private) will be the figures in column 4. The market-clearing wage for the 9,000 man-hours then rises from $3.00 to $4.00, and this rate will be paid by both the government and the private market. Several comments are in order about the phenomenon illustrated by this example.

The first thing to note is that, so long as the supply of man-hours is fixed (in this case at 9,000), some increase in wages would occur even if government demand were responsive to price. However, the increase in wages would be less pronounced if government demand were not completely inelastic. The second thing to note is that the assumption of fixed supply may be thought of as reflecting union restrictions on worker entry into the industry. As we have seen, the Davis-Bacon Act strengthens the unions' abilities to dominate certain markets, since nonunion contractors are reluctant to bid for jobs at union rates. If the government sought the lowest bidder without predetermining wage rates, additional man-hours would become available (because nonunion contractors would be drawn into the bidding), and this increased supply would help to moderate the extent of wage increases. Suppose there are no unions and 600 additional workers enter the construction industry at a wage of $3.25 an hour. In this case, government demand would raise wages to only $3.25 instead of the $4.00 of the earlier example. It is interesting to note that, when unions limit entry into the construction industry, Davis-Bacon determinations help the unions to raise private construction wage rates. A complete analysis of these issues is somewhat more involved, but the basic analytical structure of the model is made clear by this simple numerical example.

Evidence has been assembled showing that increases in government construction activity are associated with increases in union wages. Ehrenberg, Kosters, and Moskow have developed a statistical model aimed at testing the effect of increases in the fraction of Davis-Bacon contracts on the relative wages of construction workers. Their statistical analysis, which is described in greater detail in Appendix B, may be summarized as follows: when unionization and construction growth are held constant, increases in the proportion of publicly financed construction in an area result in increases in the union-scale wages of journeymen in the construction trades relative to wages of production workers in manufacturing. Ehrenberg, Kosters, and Moskow also find that increases in the proportion of publicly financed construction raise the average wage of helpers in construction trades relative to journeymen in these trades. This confirms the widely observed tendency, discussed in more detail below, of Davis-Bacon determinations to set very high relative wages for workers in apprenticeship programs, which in turn tends to discourage the use of apprentices on public construction projects. The implication of these results is that not only does the cost of construction to the government increase if it is carried out under Davis-Bacon determinations, but the cost per project increases as the total amount of such construction in an area is increased.

Finally, it should be mentioned that, even if prevailing wages reflect the average wages in the community, the requirement that these wages be paid would still favor union over open-shop contractors. If one-third of the workers of a given classification are union members, then the average wage would be higher than the average open-shop wage by an amount equal to one-third of the difference between union and nonunion wages. Even if the prevailing wage is set equal to the open-shop wage on average, but with considerable error in any one case, there would be instances in which an open-shop contractor could not perform the work without disturbing his customary wage scale.

Estimates of Increased Costs

In General Accounting Office reports and elsewhere, a number of attempts have been made to arrive at specific dollar figures for the extra costs that arise from faulty wage determinations. While these estimates vary considerably, they do provide an idea of the magnitude of the costs involved. Although an effort should be made to make such estimates precise, typically the best one can hope for is a range of figures. At any rate, for the requirements of policy, it matters very little if the true figure is one-half or twice as large as the typical estimate. The accumulated evidence points to a cost of several hundred million dollars per year. While the urgency of taking steps to eliminate the extra costs may be somewhat less if those costs are $200 million rather than $800 million, it would not fundamentally alter the policy prescription.

General Accounting Office Estimates. Early GAO studies were directed at specific cases in which there was already some presumption that improper wage determinations had been used. The percentage increase in costs should consequently be looked at as the upper bound on the correct figure for all projects covered by the Davis-Bacon Act and related legislation. In the case of seven federally funded housing projects costing a total of $15.6 million, $2.4 million (about 15 percent) was estimated to have arisen from improper wage determinations.[12] For twenty-nine federally financed construction projects costing $88 million, $9 million (about 10 percent) may have been paid in excess wages.[13] Since twenty-eight of the twenty-nine were also housing projects, a large fraction of the extra costs probably arose from the Labor Department practice, now discontinued according to department officials, of issuing residential wage determinations based on the rates for commercial buildings. According to the General Accounting Office, the federal government contributed over $1 billion annually to subsidized housing for the years 1966–1969.[14] Since the net cost to local housing authorities must be less with this federal funding (plus Davis-Bacon restrictions) than without, $1 billion represents the upper limit of yearly costs of Davis-Bacon housing determinations for this period. For fiscal 1971, two pieces of legislation alone, the National Housing Act and the United States Housing Act of 1937, had program levels of $5 billion per year.[15] If Davis-Bacon costs on federal housing amounted to 5 percent, then $250 million seems to be a reasonable estimate of the excess cost of those two programs.

In its most recent report, based on a random selection of projects, the GAO estimated that in 1967 increased construction costs due to the Davis-Bacon Act amounted to between $228 million and $513 million. In addition, the GAO estimated that the administrative costs of contractors and government agencies amounted to another $200 million per year.[16]

The 1971 Suspension. As part of a package of antiinflation measures, President Nixon suspended the Davis-Bacon Act from February 23 to

---

[12] U.S. General Accounting Office, *Construction Costs for Certain Federally Financed Housing Projects Increased Due to Inappropriate Minimum Wage Rate Determinations*, 1970, p. 17.

[13] U.S. General Accounting Office, *Need for Improved Administration of the Davis-Bacon Act Noted over a Decade of General Accounting Office Reviews*, 1971, p. 9.

[14] U.S. General Accounting Office, *Inappropriate Minimum Wage Rate Determinations*, 1970, p. 7. Not included is military housing, which was also found to have been constructed under improper determinations.

[15] Testimony of Gregory J. Ahart, director, Manpower and Welfare Division, U.S. General Accounting Office, in U.S. Congress, Senate, Subcommittee on Housing and Urban Affairs of the Committee on Banking, Housing, and Urban Affairs, *Hearings on Improved Technology and Removal of Prevailing Wage Requirements in Federally Assisted Housing*, 92d Congress, 2d session, June 1972, p. 16. The figures on program levels are being used as a proxy for the amount actually funded. According to Ahart, the latter figures were not available.

[16] U.S. General Accounting Office, *The Davis-Bacon Act Should Be Repealed*, 1979, p. 78.

March 29, 1971.[17] Construction costs had been rising faster than prices in general, and it was argued that suspension of the act would contribute to a reduction in the rate of inflation.[18] Agencies that had received bids for various projects but that had not yet awarded the contract were asked to get a second set of bids. There are some problems entailed in using the data from this historical accident. First, the second round of bids may have been affected by what contractors learned from the distribution of bids on the first round. Second, the extent of unionization would have influenced the degree to which contractors could have lowered their bids. And third, some time elapsed between the first and the second set of bids (typically about forty-five days), sufficient for higher price levels to influence the bid and, perhaps more importantly, sufficient for contractors to make substantial revisions in their estimates of the course of inflation during the construction period. For a total of seventy-six Department of Defense and General Services Administration projects with costs ranging from $2,000 to over $3 million, the average decrease in the bid was about 0.8 percent. However, this figure obscures the substantially greater changes that occurred for various classifications of projects. In particular, there may have been a tendency for the low bidder on the initial round to increase his bid if the difference between his bid and the next lowest one was fairly large. The extent of unionization may also have affected the results, since only in the case where a large fraction of construction is open shop would we expect the suspension of the act to result in lower bids. Table 14 shows the percentage change in rebids for different degrees of unionization and for differences in the extent to which the lowest bidder was less than the second lowest bidder. In the cases where the two submitted bids differed by less than 20 percent, and in states in which unionization was less than 30 percent, the new bids were 3.5 percent lower.

---

[17] For a more detailed treatment of this topic, see John P. Gould, "The Labor Component in the Cost of Housing," in U.S. Department of Housing and Urban Development, National Housing Policy Review Staff, *Housing in the Seventies: Working Papers*, vol. 1, 1976, pp. 592-94.

[18] The word "inflation" is frequently misused and certainly overused by politicians and editorial writers. In popular rhetoric, almost every economic event is somehow linked to inflation. For example, President Carter recently attributed much of the 1979 inflation to OPEC pricing policies. In fact, the most obvious and convincing explanation for the high inflation rate in the United States during the 1970s is the very high growth rate of the money supply during this period. One must be careful not to fall into the same trap in analyzing the Davis-Bacon Act. There are numerous real economic costs arising because of the act, as we have noted above. However, the act is probably not a major cause of inflation except to the extent that the government finances the increased expenditures arising from the act by more rapid expansion of the money supply.

TABLE 14

Mean Percentage Change in Bid with Davis-Bacon Act Suspended

Difference between Lowest and Next Lowest Bid	In States Less than 30% Unionized	In States More than 30% Unionized	Total
Less than 20%	− 3.476	− 0.462	− 2.66
More than 20%	3.667	14.674	5.61
Total	− 1.722	1.924	− 0.81

SOURCE: J. P. Gould, "The Labor Component in the Cost of Housing," in U.S. Department of Housing and Urban Development, National Housing Policy Review Staff, *Housing in the Seventies: Working Papers*, vol. 1, 1976, Table 5, p. 594.

Some data are also available that allow us to look at the changes that resulted from rebidding alone. Data reported by the General Services Administration indicate that for forty-one contracts for which Davis-Bacon requirements were suspended, the average low bid decreased by 5.4 percent. On another fifteen contracts for which the Davis-Bacon Act was in effect for both the first and second bid, the low bid *increased* by 2 percent, indicating that the *net* effect of the act is probably about 7.4 percent. On the basis of this evidence from the suspension, it would seem reasonable to attribute about 5 percent of the costs of a substantial fraction of projects to the Davis-Bacon Act.

The importance of breaking down the figures from the suspension is underscored by figures assembled by Thieblot and shown in Table 15. For a variety of projects on which new bids were submitted during the act's suspension, the new low bids were substantially higher, in particular for heavy construction projects. Even defenders of the Davis-Bacon Act do not contend that the act lowers construction costs or that the suspension of the act should result in higher costs. The higher bids are most reasonably interpreted as arising from other factors, such as changes in the expectations held by contractors about future prices and the bias that results from rebidding. If we assume that the categories that had higher average rebids give an indication of the strength of these influences, and that the remaining groups combine those influences *and* the effects of the Davis-Bacon Act, we can arrive at a measure of its net effect. Taking the lower figures, we find that the combined influence of factors exclusive of the Davis-Bacon Act increased the lowest bids by 3 to 4 percent. Decreases in bids, again taking the lower figures, were on the order of 1 to 3

TABLE 15

Initial Low Bids and Low Rebids Received during Davis-Bacon Act Suspension Period
(dollars in thousands)

Type of Contract	Initial Bid (1)	Rebid (2)	Decrease (1) − (2)	Percentage Decrease
By type:				
Building construction	$ 3,691	$ 3,648	$43	1.16
Metropolitan areas	485	483	2	0.41
Nonmetro areas	751	774	(23)	(3.06)
Indeterminate areas	2,455	2,391	64	2.61
Heavy construction	11,938	12,455	(517)	(4.33)
Metropolitan areas	327	354	(27)	(8.26)
Nonmetro areas	4,018	4,186	(168)	(4.18)
Indeterminate areas	7,593	7,915	(322)	(4.24)
Highway construction	2,750	2,670	80	2.91
Residential construction	12,911	12,392	519	4.02
Indeterminate type	49,284	48,901	383	0.78
By area:				
Metropolitan areas	8,798	8,350	448	5.09
Nonmetro areas	5,551	5,761	(210)	(3.78)
Indeterminate areas	66,225	65,955	270	0.41
Totals of all low bids	80,574	80,066	508	0.63

NOTE: Total number of projects was 1,263. Parentheses indicate an increase.
SOURCE: Armand J. Thieblot, Jr., *The Davis-Bacon Act*, Labor Relations and Public Policy Series, Report No. 10 (Philadelphia: University of Pennsylvania Press, 1975), Table 12, p. 93.

percent, these figures representing the combined influence of Davis-Bacon suspension and all other factors. The effect of Davis-Bacon alone on the basis of Thieblot's evidence should probably be placed in the neighborhood of 4 to 7 percent for a large fraction of projects. If a third of the projects are affected to this degree, then we can place the costs at between $500 million and $1 billion per year.[19]

---

[19] Thieblot, *Davis-Bacon Act*, p. 94, places the cost of the Davis-Bacon Act at $240 million per year. He obtains this by multiplying the 0.63 percent average decrease in the bid by the $38 billion of covered construction work. His estimate is probably an underestimate of the costs, however, since he does not take into account the effect of inflation and the tendency of rebidding to raise the average low bid, other things being equal.

It is important to emphasize that estimates of the effect of the act using these data from the suspension period are very likely to underestimate its true cost because of the short time interval (less than two months) involved. If the act were repealed, the response of nonunion contractors would be greater within six months to a year because they would have more time to adjust to the new market conditions.

The Social Effects of the Davis-Bacon Act

The requirement that wages be paid in accordance with Department of Labor determinations has several effects aside from the economic effect of raising the cost of construction to the government.

The Effect on Other Federal Programs. The Davis-Bacon Act tends to nullify the intended benefits of other federal programs. To illustrate this problem, consider the following example from Professor Yale Brozen of the University of Chicago.[20] Professor Brozen observes that the Davis-Bacon Act negates the purpose of Section 221(d)(4) of the National Housing Act, which is "to assist private industry in providing housing for low- and moderate-income families and displaced families." The National Housing Act offers subsidies to reduce interest costs in projects serving such families by having the government guarantee the loan. The guarantee in turn makes it possible to obtain a lower rate of interest. However, the high wage rates set in the Labor Department's prevailing-wage determinations on such projects reduce, and in some cases eliminate, the subsidy to these families. Professor Brozen cites the case of a developer of a high-rise apartment complex for moderate-income families in Prince George's County, Maryland. After putting up two such apartment buildings, the developer received an interest-cost subsidy for a third. In order to receive the subsidy, however, the builder was required to pay Davis-Bacon wage rates. He argued that if he were to pay these higher wages, the rentals in the new moderate-income building would be *higher* than those in the existing two buildings. Before the developer's objection was dealt with by the Wage Appeals Board, a new determination was made by the Wage Determination Division that further raised the minimum wage rates and eliminated any hope of building the low-rent housing. Fortunately for the builder and the tenants, this occurred just when the act was temporarily suspended in 1971, and the third unit was completed.

---

[20] Yale Brozen has cited a number of situations in which Davis-Bacon determinations have had damaging consequences in "The Law That Boomeranged," *Nation's Business* (April 1974), pp. 71-73.

Complaints of a similar nature were voiced by Richard C. Van Dusen, then under secretary of Housing and Urban Development, in Senate hearings in 1972. Faulty Labor Department determinations had led HUD to set up its own wage-determination staff. The concern, however, was not only the increased cost resulting from improper wage determinations. HUD provides subsidies to low-income tenants of the housing it sponsors; others pay rent in accordance with what the housing cost to construct.

> [I]f the product of a Davis-Bacon determination is the payment of wages which are higher than those which should actually prevail, that wage factor, along with other factors which typically tend to cause federally assisted projects to cost more—the paperwork and the processing time—will result in a development costing more than a conventionally produced unit with comparable or in some cases superior amenities.
>
> In this situation then the only thing that makes that HUD-assisted unit competitive is the subsidy, and when families become ineligible for subsidy because their incomes have risen, they are going to move out. The loss of these tenants will defeat the objective of having the broadest possible income mix in the project, and it will also mean that the project is really dependent upon subsidy for its economic viability which we don't regard as desirable.[21]

The Effect on Small Businesses. Most of the restrictions and requirements accompanying the Davis-Bacon Act impose a proportionally larger burden on small firms than large ones. The result of such a skewed imposition of costs is that small firms are less likely to bid on work covered by prevailing-wage legislation and, consequently, that the fraction of total construction work done by small firms will decrease. Although the additional losses in efficiency that are likely to result from an alteration of the size distribution of construction firms from its natural equilibrium may turn out to be small, it is generally considered to be bad social policy to tip the scales in favor of large firms and against small ones.

It should be remembered that union firms are typically larger than their open-shop counterparts. Thus, to the degree that the act effectively favors union over open-shop firms, more work is made available for large firms and less for small ones. In addition, if there are fixed costs for performing the paperwork required by the act,

[21] Senate, *Improved Technology and Removal of Prevailing Wage Requirements*, pp. 82-83.

large firms have a larger volume of work over which to spread those costs. And, in general, one would expect the larger firms, with their more sophisticated managerial and accounting staffs, to be able to handle these tasks more efficiently. The firms least likely to be able to fulfill the largely redundant paperwork requirements are those with fewer than twenty employees, which in 1972 accounted for 88.4 percent of all construction firms and which provided work for 38.4 percent of all construction-industry employees.[22]

The Effect on Minority Groups. Union membership practices, in conjunction with an act that shifts much government work to unions, also work to the disadvantage of minority groups. Because Davis-Bacon worker categories are so often mere copies of those found in union contracts, very few positions are available on Davis-Bacon-covered work under the categories of helper, learner, or trainee.[23] Very few union journeymen are minority-group members, and it is in the other nonjourneyman categories that most would begin their construction careers. Union apprenticeship programs limit the number of people who may enroll and often impose educational requirements that may be arbitrary. Nonunion firms, on the other hand, do not follow restrictive trade union practices. Various skill categories are recognized and there are no restrictions on, let us say, whether a laborer may use a hammer. Although nonunion contractors are not under all the restrictions in effect for union shops, during the execution of work covered by Davis-Bacon they must place all their workers in recognized categories and exclude those categories in which younger workers and members of minority groups are more likely to be found.

In fact, to be eligible for apprenticeship status under Davis-Bacon requirements, an apprentice must be enrolled in an apprenticeship program registered with the Department of Labor. Most of these programs are also under the jurisdiction of state apprenticeship councils. The management of programs is carried out by local joint apprenticeship committees composed of union and employer representatives.

For a number of possible reasons, blacks have not been enrolled in the same proportion as whites in apprenticeship programs leading

---

[22] Thieblot, *Davis-Bacon Act*, pp. 198–99.

[23] These restrictions are clearly spelled out in the Department of Labor's *Field Operations Handbook* at entry no. 15611 (9/26/69), as quoted in Thieblot, *Davis-Bacon Act*, p. 23:

> The use of helpers who use tools in assisting journeymen and who are paid below the minimum rates for journeymen is ordinarily not proper, since the apprentice is recognized as the individual who is to perform the less skilled craft work of his training period level.

to union craftsman positions.[24] Although blacks are just as likely as whites to be in various unionized skill categories in nonconstruction industries, they are more likely to be laborers and less likely to be in skilled positions in unionized construction.[25]

Why Does This Situation Persist?

In view of the costs imposed by the Davis-Bacon Act, it is natural to ask why those being hurt by the act do not do something about it. The reason is that the cards are heavily stacked against individuals who might wish to have determinations made in a way that more accurately reflects economic realities.

Consider a nonunion contractor who is bidding on a government contract in a locality where the Department of Labor has made an incorrectly high prevailing-wage determination. If that contractor decides to challenge the DOL determination, he will incur a large amount of legal and other expenses. He is not very likely to get a reversal of the DOL determination, but suppose he does. What does he gain? Actually, he gains nothing more than the right to rebid along with *everyone else* at the new wage rates. He has incurred legal costs, but has no assurance that he will get the contract. Under these circumstances individual contractors have virtually no incentive to challenge Davis-Bacon determinations. In addition, the contractor who challenges Davis-Bacon determinations may find himself subject to vandalism and other reprisals from union laborers.

If a large enough group is adversely affected by the act, and if that group can form an effective coalition, it may be possible to respond effectively to incorrect wage determinations. Recently, the Southeastern Legal Foundation challenged a Davis-Bacon determination affecting a construction contract in the state of Virginia. On May 30, 1979, the Fourth Circuit U.S. Court of Appeals ruled that DOL determinations would be reviewable in the courts from then on. While this ruling will not overcome the many Davis-Bacon abuses noted here and elsewhere, it may motivate Labor Department officials to be somewhat more careful, at least for contracts involving large amounts of state or municipal funds.

---

[24] For an account of the role of apprenticeship programs, see F. Ray Marshall and Vernon M. Briggs, *The Negro and Apprenticeship* (Baltimore: The Johns Hopkins University Press, 1967), pp. 11-45. For an account of union influence on construction employment and legal action taken against discrimination in construction unions, see William B. Gould, *Black Workers and White Unions* (Ithaca, N.Y.: Cornell University Press, 1977), pp. 281-362.

[25] See Orley Ashenfelter, "Racial Discrimination and Trade Unionism," *The Journal of Political Economy*, April/June 1972, Table 6, p. 451.

Summary

Construction-industry employment is unusual in two respects. First, a large fraction of the work force is unionized, and the wage rates of the unionized and open-shop sectors differ by substantial amounts for the different categories of workers. Second, activity in the construction industry tends to be volatile, and as a result workers in the industry are unemployed more frequently than workers in general. The higher rates of unemployment and volatility do not, however, establish any case for "wage protection." Workers are free to enter and leave this line of employment, and there is every indication that lifetime earnings (including unemployment compensation, unreported income, and the nonpecuniary benefits of more leisure time) are as high in construction as in other industries. Especially in the case of skilled workers who earn above-average incomes and who have a sophisticated understanding of the opportunities available to them, wage protection of the sort claimed for the Davis-Bacon Act is redundant.

Nor can it be argued that government construction is a special case. Government, no less than the private sector, should attempt to acquire its construction for the least cost. Since government accepts the lowest bids and does not dictate terms to either contractors or workers, there is every assurance that, for both groups, government projects will be as remunerative as private construction.

The effect of setting minimum wages that are higher than would otherwise obtain is an increase in construction costs on projects covered by the Davis-Bacon Act. Attempts to measure this increase have generally yielded estimates on the order of several hundred million dollars per year. These are the direct costs to the government that result because workers are paid unnecessary wage premiums under the act. The act also results in higher indirect costs, which include the extra costs of union construction that generally result when increased government construction in an area increases the monopoly power of the unions and thereby raises the union wage for a large fraction of private construction. Additional social costs arise as well because small, nonunion firms are more likely to be adversely affected by the act and because union employment practices and Department of Labor job classifications work to the disadvantage of younger workers and workers who are members of minority groups. Political leaders frequently express their desire to achieve efficiency and fairness in government: implementation of the GAO recommendation to repeal the Davis-Bacon Act would be a good place to start.

5
Conclusions

It appears from our survey of the literature that the Davis-Bacon Act has had a number of undesirable economic and social consequences. These consequences stem in part from the impossibility of continuously monitoring wages paid to millions of workers in dozens of construction job categories located in thousands of civil subdivisions. In part, they also stem from the ill-conceived procedures used by the Department of Labor to determine prevailing wages. While rigid, even absurd, bureaucratic practices are sometimes a necessary part of an organization's stock-in-trade, it has been amply demonstrated that the Davis-Bacon Act as administered for decades is unnecessary and costly, and constitutes a rather easily identifiable example of special-interest legislation. The central findings of our survey are as follows:

1. Nine studies of prevailing-wage determinations made by the General Accounting Office between 1962 and 1979 have shown that these determinations often establish inappropriately high minimum wages on a variety of federally financed and federally assisted projects. The validity of the GAO studies has been acknowledged by the Department of Labor on several occasions, and although Labor has said that it has halted the use of commercial building rates for residential construction, the other practices cited by GAO as causing inflated wage costs are still prevalent. The most recent GAO report was forced to conclude that "after nearly fifty years, the Department of Labor has yet to develop an effective program to issue and maintain accurate wage determinations and it may be impractical to ever do so."[1]

---

[1] U.S. General Accounting Office, *The Davis-Bacon Act Should Be Repealed,* 1979, letter of transmittal of the comptroller general.

2. The General Accounting Office classified wage determinations as "inappropriate" if they were clearly higher than would have been the case if the secretary of labor's directive on the appropriate procedures for making wage determinations had been followed. (See, for example, Tables 3 and 4.) Thus, it is important to emphasize that the determinations deemed "appropriate" by the General Accounting Office are themselves likely to be well above the rates that would obtain if the determinations were based on the rates and classifications in open shops. The 30 percent rule and the averaging rule, even when properly applied, result in wage determinations higher than the local open-shop rates.

3. Both the General Accounting Office studies and a larger sampling study by Professor D. N. Gujarati show that a very large fraction of the prevailing-wage determinations carry union scales irrespective of the location or type of construction. Data on the extent of unionization in the construction industry are incomplete, but it is clear that the fraction of determinations carrying union-scale wages is well above the fraction of unionized workers in the building trades. In its most recent study, GAO found that the Department of Labor had issued prevailing rates based on union rates in 66 percent of the determinations examined, while its own survey indicated that union rates prevailed for only 42 percent.

4. Professor Gujarati's study and the General Accounting Office reports indicate that a large fraction of the prevailing-wage determinations carried union rates from noncontiguous counties. It is not uncommon for union contractors to obtain government construction contracts in nonunion localities, thereby excluding local contractors and often local workers from these jobs. The result, at odds with the basic aim of the act, is that projects that would otherwise be carried out by local contractors and local labor are undertaken by outside firms and labor.

5. The General Accounting Office reports noted a number of instances in which wage rates from inappropriate types of construction projects were used in making prevailing-wage determinations. This inconsistency means, for example, that the determined wage rates for a highway or heavy construction project may carry the higher wage rates associated with building construction. Considerable wage differences often exist on projects that to the layman seem almost indistinguishable. In some areas not enough data from similar projects can be gathered, and the resulting wage determination is based on a sample of arbitrarily selected and unrelated projects with considerably differing wage scales.

6. The General Accounting Office also found that on-site survey data and other kinds of local wage data were often ignored in making prevailing-wage determinations. In some cases, survey data were arbitrarily altered; in others, low wages were systematically excluded. Moreover, it was found that past prevailing-wage determinations were used to make new determinations; the inclusion of these earlier determinations substantially raised the average wage rate.

7. Since the passage of the Davis-Bacon Act in 1931, many other laws have been passed that contain prevailing-wage clauses. These clauses may defeat the purpose of the primary legislation in some instances, particularly where the aim was to provide construction projects at prices lower than might prevail in the absence of government assistance. Officials of other agencies have publicly complained about the effect of Labor Department determinations on the cost of their projects and have joined contractors in appeals for lower and more realistic wage determinations.

8. By reinforcing artificial wage differentials, the Davis-Bacon Act tends to cause greater frictional unemployment in the construction trades. Construction workers appear willing to forgo current employment in order to wait for jobs paying higher union and Davis-Bacon wage rates. This has provided us with the curious combination of an excessive demand for new housing and a substantial unemployment rate among construction workers.

9. High prevailing-wage determinations appear to discourage nonunion contractors from bidding on federal construction jobs. This means that union contractors face less competition, that the government has to pay a premium for construction work, and that the bargaining power of unionized construction workers is strengthened substantially. Excluding nonunion contractors from a substantial part of the construction market also has undesirable economic consequences for minority groups and for younger workers, who are more likely to find employment in the nonunion sector of the construction industry.

10. Job classifications in Labor Department determinations usually conform to those established by the building trade unions. This implies that no helpers and only apprentices from the union-dominated training programs are specified. Apprentice classifications tend to carry the higher union rates, and this, together with the classification restrictions, results in curtailed use of apprentices and helpers on Davis-Bacon projects, even when they are undertaken by open-shop contractors.

11. Prevailing-wage determinations in general (and the practice of basing new determinations on old ones in particular) tend to freeze

wage differentials irrespective of shifts in demand. This interferes with the workings of the labor market as a resource-allocation mechanism and may prevent the proper flow of workers into different jobs and areas.

12. On the basis of evidence from the 1971 suspension and from the various General Accounting Office reports, it seems reasonable to place the cost of the Davis-Bacon Act at between $0.5 billion and $1 billion per year. This is an estimate of the government's extra costs, which arise because: (1) union labor is used on projects where less highly paid nonunion labor would otherwise have performed the work; (2) nonunion labor must be paid more while working on covered projects than it ordinarily receives; (3) administrative costs to contractors are included in bids; and (4) administrative costs are imposed on the Department of Labor and other government agencies. To the extent that government-induced demand for union labor increases union monopoly power, the Davis-Bacon Act may also result in higher construction costs for union construction in the private sector.

APPENDIX A

An Algebraic Model of the Effects
of Prevailing-Wage Laws

This appendix provides a simple analytical device for evaluating the effect of Davis-Bacon on average construction industry wages. The model developed here highlights many of the factors that appear to be essential to an understanding of the economics of the Davis-Bacon Act and provides a formal structure within which differences of judgment and fact can be compared and examined.

The construction industry is thought of as divided into a union and a nonunion sector. The number u ($0 \leqslant u \leqslant 1$) stands for the fraction of unionized construction workers and $(1 - u)$ is the fraction of nonunion construction workers. Wage rates are represented by w_u and w_c for union and nonunion workers respectively. From such information the average construction industry wage rate, A_0, may be calculated as follows:

$$A_0 = u\, w_u + (1 - u)\, w_c \tag{1}$$

If the government shifts a fraction of construction contracts, g, from the union to the nonunion sector, the average wage becomes

$$A_1 = (u - g)\, w_u + [(1 - u) + g]\, w_c \tag{2}$$

The difference in average wages attributable to the fraction g of government contracts that go to the union sector is, therefore,

$$A_0 - A_1 = g(w_u - w_c) \tag{3}$$

This difference will be positive (i.e., average wages are increased by government spending in the union sector), if the union rate, w_u, exceeds the nonunion rate, w_c. The difference can be expressed in percentage terms as follows:

$$\frac{A_0 - A_1}{A_1} = \frac{g(r - 1)}{1 + (u - g)\,(r - 1)} \tag{4}$$

where $r = \dfrac{w_u}{w_c}$, the ratio of union to nonunion wages.

69

Inspection of equation (4) shows that the percentage increase in average construction-industry wages attributable to government spending in the union sector will be larger, the larger the fraction g and the larger the ratio of union to nonunion wages, r.

This kind of straightforward calculation glosses over several significant problems. It assumes that supply is completely elastic in the nonunion sector and that wages will be maintained in the union sector despite the loss in government demand. If one believes that the shift in government demand automatically shifts the corresponding number of workers from the union to the nonunion sector, these assumptions are justified. However, while some shifting of this nature will no doubt occur, it seems unlikely that shifts in labor supply will follow government demand on a one-for-one basis. There are several reasons for this. First, union workers may be willing to accept some unemployment rather than a cut in wages. Moreover, it is possible that there will be some reduction in union wages to stimulate private demand in the union sector that will partially offset the loss of government demand. It is also possible that the shift in government demand from union to nonunion labor is accompanied to some extent by "geographical" shifts in demand. Such a geographical shift need not occur because the government changes the location of its construction activities. It may occur because union labor which formerly was imported into a nonunion region would no longer be imported because such importations look less attractive at the lower, nonunion wage rates.

If union labor does not shift fully into the nonunion sector following the shift in government purchases, the above measure of the change in average wages, equation (4), must be modified to allow for the accompanying changes in relative wages and in employment in the union and nonunion sectors. To account for such changes, it is desirable to derive a rather general measure of the effect of government spending on average wage rates, which then can be used to examine specific cases of interest.

The government's demand for construction projects is assumed to be completely price inelastic. While budget constraints and the use of cost-benefit analysis in government planning means that this assumption is not literally true, it is likely to be a very good approximation for the questions examined in this paper. Given that government contracts are price inelastic, the effect of a shift in the contracts from the union to the nonunion sector is shown in diagrams on the next page.

Initially, there are N_u man-hours (including government demand) in the union sector and N_c man-hours in the nonunion sector. The

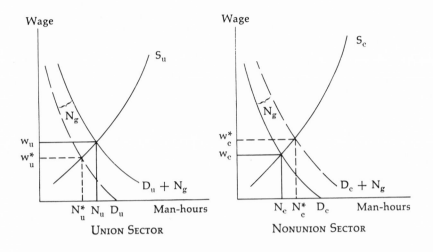

UNION SECTOR   NONUNION SECTOR

demand curves D_u and D_c represent nongovernment demand in each sector. The variables w_u and w_c are the initial wages which are determined by the intersection of the demand curves (including government demand) with their respective supply curves S_u and S_c. The inelastic demand of the government for N_g man-hours is shown initially as a horizontal shift of the union sector demand curve. If the government shifts its demand to the nonunion sector, the union sector demand curve moves to the left and the nonunion demand curve to the right, thereby establishing new equilibrium wages w_u^* and w_c^* (where $w_u^* < w_u$ and $w_c^* > w_c$) and new equilibrium man-hours N_u^* and N_c^* (where $N_u^* < N_u$ and $N_c^* > N_c$).

It is interesting to see how the inelastic demand of the government in a sector serves to raise wages for nongovernmental demand in that sector. It is because of this phenomenon that unions are able to use government contracts as a device to raise wages on *nongovernment* contracts. Thus, it can be seen how Davis-Bacon determinations "spill over" to the private sector. Of course, there is also "spillover" to private construction in the nonunion sector when government contracts are moved there. The following analysis will be helpful in unscrambling and comparing these effects.

Before going to the analysis of the above shift, we consider the general problem of the effect on wages and on employment of a change in price-inelastic demand in a market. In equilibrium, these conditions obtain:

$$q_d = I + f(p) \tag{5}$$

$$q_s = s(p) \tag{6}$$

71

$$q_s = q_d = q_e \tag{7}$$

Condition (5) is the market demand, where I represents the inelastic demand and $f(p)$ the price-dependent demand. Condition (6) is market supply, and condition (7) establishes the market-clearing quantity and, hence, price. Condition (7) can be used to eliminate q_d and q_s from (5) and (6) so that

$$I + f(p) = s(p) \tag{8}$$

Differentiating (8) with respect to I we obtain

$$1 + f'(p)\frac{dp}{dI} = s'(p)\frac{dp}{dI}$$

Rearranging,

$$dp = \frac{dI}{s'(p) - f'(p)}$$

Multiplying both sides by $1/p$ and multiplying the right-hand side by $(1/q_e)/(1/q_e) = 1$

$$\frac{dp}{p} = \frac{dI/q_e}{\eta_s - \eta_d} \tag{9}$$

where η_s and η_d are, respectively, the supply and the demand price elasticities.[1] Thus, equation (9) says that the percentage change in price is equal to the increase in inelastic demand as a percent of the initial equilibrium quantity divided by the difference between supply elasticity and demand elasticity. Since the elasticities are calculated at the initial equilibrium, this equation is an approximation that is equivalent to assuming linear supply and demand curves over the range of the shift. The percentage change in the equilibrium quantity is then

$$\frac{d_q}{q_e} = \frac{dI}{q_e}\left(1 + \frac{\eta_d}{\eta_s - \eta_d}\right) \tag{10}$$

Equations (9) and (10) can be used to evaluate the shifts illustrated in the above diagrams. Before the government shifts its demand to the nonunion sector, the average construction industry wage is

$$A_0 = \frac{w_u N_u + w_c N_c}{N_u + N_c} = u w_u + c w_c$$

where u is the fraction of man-hours in the union sector and $c = 1 - u$ is the fraction of man-hours in the nonunion sector. Now let $\dot{\triangle} w_c$

---

[1] Demand elasticity is the percentage change in quantity demanded divided by the percentage change in price. The supply elasticity is the percentage change in quantity supplied divided by the percentage change in price.

and $\dot{\triangle} w_u$ be the percentage change in nonunion and in union wage rates, respectively. Then, using (9) and (10), the new equilibrium values of wages and employment in each sector can be written

$$w_c^* = w_c(1 + \dot{\triangle} w_c) = w_c \left(1 + \frac{N_g}{N_c} \frac{1}{\eta_s^c - \eta_d^c} \right) \qquad (11)$$

$$N_c^* = N_c(1 + \eta_d^c \dot{\triangle} w_c) + N_g = N_c \left[1 + \left(\frac{N_g}{N_c} \right) \frac{\eta_d^c}{\eta_s^c - \eta_d^c} \right] + N_g \qquad (12)$$

$$w_u^* = w_u(1 + \dot{\triangle} w_u) = w_u \left(1 - \left(\frac{N_g}{N_u - N_g} \right) \frac{1}{\eta_s^u - \eta_d^u} \right) \qquad (13)$$

$$N_u^* = (N_u - N_g)(1 + \eta_d^u \dot{\triangle} w_u)$$
$$= (N_u - N_g) \left(1 - \left(\frac{N_g}{N_u - N_g} \right) \frac{\eta_d^u}{\eta_s^u - \eta_d^u} \right) \qquad (14)$$

where η_s^c, η_d^c are the supply and demand elasticities in the nonunion sector and η_s^u, η_d^u are the supply and demand elasticities in the union sector. Following the shift in government demand, the average wage rate becomes

$$A_1 = \frac{w_c^* N_c^* + w_u^* N_u^*}{N_c^* + N_u^*} \qquad (15)$$

Using equations (11), (12), (13), and (14), and dividing through by N_c, (15) may be expressed in terms of the initial proportions as

$$A_1 = \frac{w_c \left[1 + \frac{g}{c} \lambda_c \right] \left[1 + \frac{g}{c} (1 + \eta_d^c \lambda_c) \right] + w_u \left(\frac{u-g}{c} \right) \left(1 - \frac{g}{u-g} \lambda_u \right) \left(1 - \frac{g}{u-g} \eta_d^u \lambda_u \right)}{\left[1 + \frac{g}{c} \left((1 + \eta_d^c \lambda_c) \right) \right] + \frac{u-g}{c} \left(1 - \frac{g}{u-g} \lambda_u \eta_d^u \right)} \qquad (16)$$

where $\lambda_c = \frac{1}{\eta_s^c - \eta_d^c}$ and $\lambda_u = \frac{1}{\eta_s^u - \eta_d^u}$

It is possible to derive specific cases from this general expression. For example, equation (2) is equivalent to the assumption that both supply elasticities are infinite (completely elastic) since union labor shifts freely into the nonunion sector. This means that λ_u and λ_c are zero and (16) becomes

$$A_1 = \frac{w_c \left(1 + \frac{g}{c} \right) + w_u \left(\frac{u-g}{c} \right)}{1 + \frac{g}{c} + \frac{u-g}{c}} = w_c(c + g) + w_u(u - g) \qquad (17)$$

Since $c = 1 - u$, this is the same expression as (2). At another extreme, one might assume that the union accepts whatever wage

73

cut is necessary to maintain union employment at the pre-shift level N_u. In this case, $\eta_s^u = 0$ so $\lambda_u = -1/\eta_d^u$ and (16) becomes

$$A_1 = \frac{w_c\left[1 + \frac{g}{c}\lambda_c\right]\left[1 + \frac{g}{c}(1 + \eta_d^c\lambda_c)\right] + w_u\left(1 + \frac{g}{u-g}\right)\left(\frac{u-g}{c}\right)\left[1 + \frac{g}{u-g}\frac{1}{\eta_d^u}\right]}{\left[1 + \frac{g}{c}(1 + \eta_d^c\lambda_c)\right] + \frac{u-g}{c}\left(1 + \frac{g}{u-g}\right)} \quad (18)$$

Equation (18) is more complex than (17) because there are changes in nonunion employment (and hence in total employment in construction) and because there are wage changes in both sectors. One must use some caution with (18) because if it is interpreted in a strictly mechanical manner it would be possible in some cases to have the union wage rate drop below the nonunion rate. Since this is nonsense from an economic point of view, it would be necessary to drop the assumption of complete inelasticity of union supply if it implies a "negative" differential in the empirical estimates.

This raises another, more realistic, question, however. One might wish to think of the union supply curve as a function of the *difference* in union and nonunion wage rates, as well as the union rate itself. No attempt is made here to build this possibility into a formal model, but it is worth keeping this idea in mind when interpreting the results of equation (18). In particular, if the differential between union and nonunion rates gets very small, it is probably best to drop the assumption of complete inelasticity of supply.

A major advantage of equation (18) is that it focuses attention on economic variables that play a key role in determining the effect of the Davis-Bacon Act. It is very difficult to get any good data on the parameters—we need to have values for four elasticities; the proportion of man-hours in union, government, and nonunion construction work; and the differential between union and nonunion wages.

APPENDIX B

The Ehrenberg, Kosters, and Moskow Analysis

This appendix briefly summarizes the preliminary work by Ehrenberg, Kosters, and Moskow to estimate the effect of Davis-Bacon type contracts on the relative wages of construction workers. The basic statistical model they examined is [1]

$$R = a_0 + a_1 U + a_2 PUB + a_3 G$$

R is a measure of the relative wage of unionized construction workers, U is the extent of unionization in nonresidential construction, PUB is the proportion of nonresidential construction that is publicly financed or assisted, and G is a measure of recent growth in construction activity. All of these variables are logarithms of the basic data.

The coefficients a_1, a_2, a_3—measuring the relationship of U, PUB, and G to relative union wages R—are unknown and must be estimated. For example, if a_2 is found to be positive, it implies that increases in the proportion of nonresidential construction that is publicly financed increase union wage rates relative to other wages.

It is difficult to get precise data on the relevant variables in this equation, and the authors provide a detailed discussion of the conceptual difficulties inherent in the measures they used. The reader who is interested in a detailed discussion of these problems is referred to the Ehrenberg-Kosters-Moskow paper. We provide a brief description of the data here.

The data for all variables were obtained from a cross-section of sixty-two metropolitan areas with populations of over 100,000. The authors used three measures of relative union wage rates, but we will focus on only one of them here. The variable R is the average union

---

[1] Ronald G. Ehrenberg, "The Economic Impact of Davis-Bacon Type Legislation: An Econometric Study," unpublished paper, March 1971.

wage scale of journeymen in the building trades divided by the average hourly earnings of local production workers in manufacturing.[2] These wage data were obtained from Bureau of Labor Statistics publications and were averaged over a three-year period (1967, 1968, and 1969) in an attempt to avoid the effects of different timings of contract expirations over the sixty-two metropolitan areas. The geographical coverage of the two wage series is not identical (city vs. Standard Metropolitan Statistical Area).

The measure of unionization in each area, U, is the ratio of building-trade union membership in each area to average nonresidential construction employment in the SMSA. Details on the construction of this variable can be found in the Ehrenberg-Kosters-Moskow paper. PUB is the proportion of the value of nonresidential construction in the SMSA which appeared to be either publicly financed or assisted. This variable is obtained from unpublished data of the F. W. Dodge Company on the value of construction contract awards by city and by type of construction. The variable is defined to include construction activity defined as public by F. W. Dodge and transportation-related building (such as airplane hangars) and also utilities and transportation-related nonbuilding construction. The authors believe that the bulk of these additional construction activities are covered by legislation that contains Davis-Bacon type prevailing-wage determination clauses. In order to get a measure of the "permanent" impact of Davis-Bacon determinations, these data were averaged over the three-year period 1965–1967.

G is the growth of construction in the area and is measured as the percentage change of the average value of construction in 1965–1967 over the average value of construction in 1961–1964.

Using standard statistical regression techniques, the authors estimated several equations. The following equation is a typical example of the results:[3]

$$R = 2.184 + 0.678\ PUB + 0.121\ U + 0.243\ G$$

This equation may be interpreted as follows: when the proportion of publicly financed construction in an area (i.e., PUB) rises by 10 percent, union wages of journeymen in construction rise by about

---

[2] The authors also used (a) the ratio of building-trade helpers' average union wage scales to average hourly earnings of manufacturing production workers, and (b) the ratio of building-trade helpers' average union wage scales to journeymen's average union wage scales in other regressions.

[3] The t-ratios are 5.01, 2.44, 1.19, and 2.52 for the constant, PUB, U, and G, respectively. The squared multiple correlation coefficient is 0.259. The authors' other regressions provided generally similar kinds of results.

6.8 percent relative to wages of production workers in manufacturing.[4] The effect of increases in the fraction of publicly financed construction appears to be stronger than the effect of increases in construction activity—a 10 percent increase in G raises relative union wages of journeymen in the building trades by about 2.4 percent.

Among the other regressions reported by Ehrenberg, Kosters, and Moskow is the following:[5]

$$RW3 = -0.182 + 0.118\ PUB + 0.002\ U + 0.065\ G$$

where $RW3$ is the ratio of building-trade helpers' average union wage scales to building-trade journeymen in each area. The coefficient on PUB in this equation, 0.118, indicates that a 10 percent increase in the fraction of publicly financed or assisted construction raises the average wages of helpers by about 1.2 percent relative to journeymen in the building trades. This increase probably results from the tendency of Davis-Bacon determinations to set very high relative wage rates for workers in apprenticeship-training programs, as has been noted by Professor Brozen.[6]

The findings of Ehrenberg, Kosters, and Moskow have to be interpreted with some caution. The authors note that their estimates are only tentative, given the crude nature of the data and the limited geographic coverage of the sample. They also point out that there is no presumption that their model contains all the relevant variables. Indeed, the squared multiple correlation coefficients of between 0.2 and 0.4 suggest that additional explanatory variables might successfully be incorporated into the model.

It is not easy to ascertain the precise impact of Davis-Bacon determinations from these results, since it is possible that increases in public construction per se (i.e., in the absence of prevailing-wage determinations) may lead to somewhat similar results. This problem is handled in part by the use of the control variable G, but there is some danger of multicollinearity between PUB and G (and also between PUB and U). There is also the danger, as the authors point out, that any "spillover" of wages in construction to wages in other indus-

---

[4] The coefficients of PUB, U, and G are elasticities, since all variables are measured in logarithms.

[5] The t-ratios are 1.78, 1.78, 0.06 and 2.83 for the constant term, PUB, U, and G, respectively. The squared coefficient of multiple correlation is 0.195.

[6] Yale Brozen, "The Davis-Bacon Act: How to Load the Dice against Yourself," in U.S. Congress, Senate, Subcommittee on Housing and Urban Affairs of the Committee on Banking, Housing, and Urban Affairs, *Hearings on Improved Technology and Removal of Prevailing Wage Requirements in Federally Assisted Housing*, 92d Congress, 2d session, June 1972, pp. 397-400.

tries (such as manufacturing) can result in a downward bias in the estimate of the *relative* impact of *PUB, U,* and *G.*

Despite such ambiguities, these initial findings are in accordance with the studies of the General Accounting Office and with the work of Professor Gujarati, and the accumulated evidence points quite strongly in the direction that Davis-Bacon determinations (and determinations of related legislation) exert a powerful upward pressure on relative wages in the construction industry. This upward movement appears to take place directly in public construction and indirectly in private construction through the increased bargaining power which unions derive from the prevailing-wage laws.

APPENDIX C

The Davis-Bacon Act (as Amended)

40 U.S. CODE, § 276

a. Rate of wages for laborers and mechanics

(a) The advertised specifications for every contract in excess of $2,000, to which the United States or the District of Columbia is a party, for construction, alteration, and/or repair, including painting and decorating, of public buildings or public works of the United States or the District of Columbia within the geographic limits of the States of the Union, or the District of Columbia, and which requires or involves the employment of mechanics and/or laborers shall contain a provision stating the minimum wages to be paid various classes of laborers and mechanics which shall be based upon the wages that will be determined by the Secretary of Labor to be prevailing for the corresponding classes of laborers and mechanics employed on projects of a character similar to the contract work in the city, town, village, or other civil subdivision of the State, in which the work is to be performed, or in the District of Columbia if the work is to be performed there; and every contract based upon these specifications shall contain a stipulation that the contractor or his subcontractor shall pay all mechanics and laborers employed directly upon the site of the work, unconditionally and not less often than once a week, and without subsequent deduction or rebate on any account, the full amounts accrued at time of payment, computed at wage rates not less than those stated in the advertised specifications, regardless of any contractual relationship which may be alleged to exist between the contractor or subcontractor and such laborers and mechanics, and that the scale of wages to be paid shall be posted by the contractor in a prominent and easily accessible place at the site of the work; and the further stipulation that there may be withheld from the contractor so much of accrued payments as may be considered necessary by the contracting officer to pay to laborers and mechanics employed by the contractor or any subcontractor on the work the difference between the rates of wages required by the contract to be paid laborers and mechanics on the work and the rates of wages received by such laborers and mechanics and not refunded to the contractor, subcontractors, or their agents.

(b) As used in sections 276a to 276a–5 of this title the term "wages," "scale of wages," "wage rates," "minimum wages," and "prevailing wages" shall include—

(1) the basic hourly rate of pay; and
(2) the amount of—

>(A) the rate of contribution irrevocably made by a contractor or subcontractor to a trustee or to a third person pursuant to a fund, plan, or program; and

>(B) the rate of costs to the contractor or subcontractor which may be reasonably anticipated in providing benefits to laborers and mechanics pursuant to an enforceable commitment to carry out a financially responsible plan or program which was communicated in writing to the laborers and mechanics affected,

for medical or hospital care, pensions on retirement or death, compensation for injuries or illness resulting from occupational activity, or insurance to provide any of the foregoing, for unemployment benefits, life insurance, disability and sickness insurance, or accident insurance, for vacation and holiday pay, for defraying costs of apprenticeship or other similar programs, or for other bona fide fringe benefits, but only where the contractor or subcontractor is not required by other Federal, State, or local law to provide any of such benefits:

Provided, That the obligation of a contractor or subcontractor to make payment in accordance with the prevailing wage determinations of the Secretary of Labor, insofar as sections 276a to 276a–5 of this title and other Acts incorporating sections 276a to 276a–5 of this title by reference are concerned may be discharged by the making of payments in cash, by the making of contributions of a type referred to in paragraph (2) (A), or by the assumption of an enforceable commitment to bear the costs of a plan or program of a type referred to in paragraph (2) (B), or any combination thereof, where the aggregate of any such payments, contributions, and costs is not less than the rate of pay described in paragraph (1) plus the amount referred to in paragraph (2).

In determining the overtime pay to which the laborer or mechanic is entitled under any Federal law, his regular or basic hourly rate of pay (or other alternative rate upon which premium rate of overtime compensation is computed) shall be deemed to be the rate computed under paragraph (1), except that where the amount of payments, contributions, or costs incurred with respect to him exceeds the prevailing wage applicable to him under sections 276a to 276a–5 of this title, such regular or basic hourly rate of pay (or such other alternative rate) shall be arrived at by deducting from the amount of payments, contributions, or costs actually incurred with respect to him, the amount of contributions or costs of the types described in paragraph (2) actually incurred with respect to him, or the amount determined under paragraph (2) but not actually paid, whichever amount is the greater.

a–1. Termination of work on failure to pay agreed wages; completion of work by Government

Every contract within the scope of sections 276a to 276a–5 of this title shall contain the further provision that in the event it is found by the contracting officer that any laborer or mechanic employed by the contractor or any subcontractor directly on the site of the work covered by the contract has been or is being paid a rate of wages less than the rate of wages required by the contract to be paid as aforesaid, the Government may, by written notice to the contractor, terminate his right to proceed with the work or such part of the work as to which there has been a failure to pay said required wages and to prosecute the work to completion by contract or otherwise, and the contractor and his sureties shall be liable to the Government for any excess costs occasioned the Government thereby.

a–2. Payment of wages by Comptroller General from withheld payments; listing contractors violating contracts

(a) The Comptroller General of the United States is authorized and directed to pay directly to laborers and mechanics from any accrued payments withheld under the terms of the contract any wages found to be due laborers and mechanics pursuant to sections 276a to 276a–5 of this title; and the Comptroller General of the United States is further authorized and is directed to distribute a list to all departments of the Government giving the names of persons or firms whom he has found to have disregarded their obligations to employees and subcontractors. No contract shall be awarded to the persons or firms appearing on this list or to any firm, corporation, partnership, or association in which such persons or firms have an interest until three years have elapsed from the date of publication of the list containing the names of such persons or firms.

(b) If the accrued payments withheld under the terms of the contract, as aforesaid, are insufficient to reimburse all the laborers and mechanics, with respect to whom there has been a failure to pay the wages required pursuant to sections 276a to 276a–5 of this title, such laborers and mechanics shall have the right of action and/or of intervention against the contractor and his sureties conferred by law upon persons furnishing labor or materials, and in such proceedings it shall be no defense that such laborers and mechanics accepted or agreed to accept less than the required rate of wages or voluntarily made refunds.

a–3. Effect on other Federal laws

Sections 276a to 276a–5 of this title shall not be construed to supersede or impair any authority otherwise granted by Federal law to provide for the establishment of specific wage rates.

a–4. Effective date of sections 276a to 276a–5

Sections 276a to 276a–5 of this title shall take effect thirty days after August 30, 1935, but shall not affect any contract then existing or any other contract that may thereafter be entered into pursuant to invitations for bids that are outstanding on August 30, 1935.

a–5. Suspension of sections 276a to 276a–5 during emergency

In the event of a national emergency the President is authorized to suspend the provisions of sections 276a to 276a–5 of this title.

a–6. Appropriation

a–7. Application of sections 276a to 276a–5 to contracts entered into without regard to section 5 of Title 41

The fact that any contract authorized by any Act is entered into without regard to section 5 of Title 41, or upon a cost-plus-a-fixed-fee basis or otherwise without advertising for proposals, shall not be construed to render inapplicable the provisions of sections 276a to 276a–5 of this title, if such Act would otherwise be applicable to such contract.

APPENDIX D

Statutes Requiring Davis-Bacon Act
Wage Determinations

1. Federal-Aid Highway Act of 1956 (sec. 108(b), 70 Stat. 378, re-codified at 72 Stat. 895; 23 U.S.C. 113(a), as amended); see particularly the amendments in the Federal-Aid Highway Act of 1968 (Public Law 90-495, 62 Stat. 815).

2. National Housing Act (sec. 212 added to c. 847, 48 Stat. 1246 by sec. 14, 53 Stat. 807; 12 U.S.C. 1715(c)); repeatedly amended.

3. Federal Airport Act (sec. 15, 60 Stat. 178; 49 U.S.C. 1114(b)).

4. Housing Act of 1949 (sec. 109, 63 Stat. 419, as amended; 42 U.S.C. 1459).

5. School Survey and Construction Act of 1950 (sec. 101, 72 Stat. 551, 20 U.S.C. 636(b)(1)(E), Public Law 85-620).

6. Defense Housing and Community Facilities and Services Act of 1951 (sec. 310, 65 Stat. 307, 42 U.S.C. 15921).

7. U.S. Housing Act of 1937 (sec. 16, 50 Stat. 896, as amended; 42 U.S.C. 1416).

8. Federal Civil Defense Act of 1950 (sec. 3(c), 72 Stat. 533; 50 U.S.C. App. 2281, Public Law 85-606).

9. Health Professions Educational Assistance Act of 1963 (sec. 2(a), 77 Stat. 164; 42 U.S.C. 292d(c)(4) and 42 U.S.C. 293a(c)(5), Public Law 88-129).

10. Mental Retardation Facilities Construction Act (sec. 101, 122, 135; 77 Stat. 282, 284, 288, 42 U.S.C. 295(a)(2)(D), 2662(5), 2675(a)(5), Public Law 88-164).

SOURCE: U.S. General Accounting Office, *The Davis-Bacon Act Should Be Repealed*, 1979, Appendix III.

11. Community Mental Health Centers Act (sec. 205, 77 Stat. 292; 42 U.S.C. 2685(a)(5), Public Law 88-164).

12. Higher Educational Facilities Act of 1963 (sec. 403, 77 Stat. 379; 20 U.S.C. 753, Public Law 88-204).

13. Vocational Educational Act of 1963 (sec. 7, 77 Stat. 408; 20 U.S.C. 35f, Public Law 88-210).

14. Library Services and Construction Act (sec. 7(a), 78 Stat. 13; 20 U.S.C. 355c(a)(4), Public Law 88-269).

15. Urban Mass Transportation Act of 1964 (sec. 10, 78 Stat. 307; 49 U.S.C. 1609, Public Law 88-365).

16. Economic Opportunity Act of 1964 (sec. 607, 78 Stat. 532; 42 U.S.C. 2947, Public Law 88-452).

17. Hospital Survey and Construction Act, as amended by the Hospital and Medical Facilities Amendments of 1964 (sec. 605(a)(5), 78 Stat. 453; 42 U.S.C. 291e(a)(5), Public Law 88-443).

18. Housing Act of 1964 (adds sec. 516(f) to Housing Act of 1949 by sec. 503, 78 Stat. 797; 42 U.S.C. 1486(f), Public Law 88-560).

19. Commercial Fisheries Research and Development Act of 1964 (sec. 7, 78 Stat. 199; 16 U.S.C. 779e(b), Public Law 88-309).

20. Nurse Training Act of 1964 (sec. 2, 78 Stat. 909; 42 U.S.C. 296a (b)(5), Public Law 88-581).

21. Appalachian Regional Development Act of 1965 (sec. 402, 79 Stat. 21; 40 U.S.C. App. 402, Public Law 90-103).

22. Act to provide Financial Assistance for Local Educational Agencies in areas affected by Federal activities (64 Stat. 1100, as amended by sec. 2, 79 Stat. 33; 20 U.S.C. 2411, Public Law 89-10).

23. Elementary and Secondary Education Act of 1965 (sec. 308, 79 Stat. 44; 20 U.S.C. 848, Public Law 89-10).

24. Cooperative Research Act of 1966 (sec. 4(c), added by sec. 403, 79 Stat. 46; U.S.C. 332a(c), Public Law 89-750).

25. Housing Act of 1961 (sec. 707, added by sec. 907, 79 Stat. 496; 42 U.S.C. 1500c-3, Public Law 86-117).

26. Housing and Urban Development Act of 1965 (sec. 707, 79 Stat. 492; 42 U.S.C. 3107, Public Law 89-117).

27. Public Works and Economic Development Act of 1965 (sec. 712, 79 Stat. 575; 42 U.S.C. 3222, Public Law 89-136).

28. National Foundation on the Arts and Humanities Act of 1965 (sec. 5(k), 79 Stat. 846; 20 U.S.C. 954(k), Public Law 89-209).

29. Federal Water Pollution Control Act, as amended by sec. 4(g) of the Water Quality Act of 1965 (79 Stat. 910; 33 U.S.C. 466e(g), Public Law 89-234).

30. Heart Disease, Cancer, and Stroke Amendments of 1965 (sec. 904, as added by sec. 2, 79 Stat. 928; 42 U.S.C. 299d(b)(4), Public Law 89-239).

31. National Capital Transportation Act of 1965 (sec. 3(b)(4), 79 Stat. 644; 40 U.S.C. 682(b)(4), Public Law 89-173). Note: Repealed December 9, 1969, and labor standards incorporated in sec. 1-1431 of the District of Columbia Code.

32. Vocational Rehabilitation Act (sec. 12(b), added by sec. 3, 79 Stat. 1284; 29 U.S.C. 41a(b)(4), Public Law 89-333).

33. Medical Library Assistance Act of 1965 (sec. 2, adding sec. 393 of the Public Health Service Act, 79 Stat. 1060; 42 U.S.C. 280b-3 (b)(3), Public Law 89-291).

34. Solid Waste Disposal Act (sec. 207, 79 Stat. 1000; 42 U.S.C. 3256, Public Law 89-272).

35. National Technical Institute for the Deaf Act (sec. 5(b)(5), 70 Stat. 126; 20 U.S.C. 684(b)(5), Public Law 89-36).

36. Demonstration Cities and Metropolitan Development Act of 1966 (sec. 110, 311, 503, 1003, 80 Stat. 1259, 1270, 1277, 1284; 42 U.S.C. 3310; 12 U.S.C. 1715c; 42 U.S.C. 1416, Public Law 89-745).

37. Model Secondary School for the Deaf Act (sec. 4, 80 Stat. 1028, Public Law 89-695).

38. Delaware River Basin Compact (sec. 15.1, 75 Stat. 714, Public Law 87-328), considered a statute for purposes of the plan.

39. Alaska Purchase Centennial (sec. 2(b), 80 Stat. 8, Public Law 89-375).

40. Highway Speed Ground Transportation Study (sec. 6(b), 79 Stat. 895; 49 U.S.C. 1636(b), Public Law 89-220).

41. Allied Health Professions Personnel Training Act of 1966 (80 Stat. 1222; 42 U.S.C. 295h(b)(2)(E), Public Law 89-751).

42. Air Quality Act of 1967 (sec. 307 added by sec. 2, 81 Stat. 506; 42 U.S.C. 1957j-3, Public Law 90-148).

43. Elementary and Secondary Education Amendments of 1967 (81 Stat. 819; 20 U.S.C. 880b-6, Public Law 90-247).

44. Vocational Rehabilitation Amendments of 1967 (81 Stat. 252, 29 U.S.C. 42a(c)(3), Public Law 90-391).

45. National Visitors Center Facilities Act of 1968 (sec. 110, 82 Stat. 45; 40 U.S.C. 808, Public Law 90-264).

46. Juvenile Delinquency Prevention and Control Act of 1968 (sec. 133, 82 Stat. 469; 42 U.S.C. 3843, Public Law 90-445).

47. New Communities Act of 1968 (sec. 410 of Public Law 90-448, 82 Stat. 516; 42 U.S.C. 3909).

48. Alcoholic and Narcotic Addict Rehabilitation Amendments of 1968 (sec. 243(d) added by sec. 301, 82 Stat. 1008; 42 U.S.C. 2688h(d), Public Law 88-164).

49. Vocational Education Amendments of 1968 (sec. 106 added by sec. 101(b), 82 Stat. 1069; 20 U.S.C. 1246, Public Law 90-576).

50. Postal Reorganization Act (39 U.S.C. 410(b)(4)(c), Public Law 91-375).

51. Developmental Disabilities Services and Facilities Construction Amendments of 1970 (sec. 135(a)(5), 84 Stat. 1316; 42 U.S.C. 2675, Public Law 91-517).

52. Rail Passenger Service Act of 1970 (sec. 405(d), 84 Stat. 1327; 45 U.S.C. 565, Public Law 91-518).

53. Housing and Urban Development Act of 1970 (sec. 707(a) and (b), 84 Stat. 1770; Public Law 91-609, 42 U.S.C. 1500c-3).

54. Airport and Airway Development Act of 1970 (sec. 22(b), 84 Stat. 219; Public Law 91-258, 41 U.S.C. 1722(b)); this act provides for wage determination by the secretary of labor, but does not subject the act to Reorganization Plan No. 14.

55. Elementary and Secondary Education Amendments (sec. 423, 84 Stat. 121; Public Law 91-230, 20 U.S.C. 1231 et seq.).

56. Housing Act of 1959 (73 Stat. 681, 12 U.S.C. 1701q(c)(3), Public Law 86-372).

57. Housing Act of 1950 (64 Stat. 78, 12 U.S.C. 1749a(f)).

58. Area Redevelopment Act of 1961 (75 Stat. 61, 42 U.S.C. 2518, Public Law 87-27).

59. Mental Retardation Facilities and Community Mental Health Centers Construction Act Amendments of 1965 (79 Stat. 429, 20 U.S.C. 618(g), Public Law 89-105).

60. Veterans Nursing Home Care Act of 1964 (78 Stat. 502, 38 U.S.C. 5035(a)(8), Public Law 88-450).

61. Education Amendments of 1972 (86 Stat. 331, Public Law 92-318).

62. Juvenile Delinquency Prevention and Control Act of 1968, amendment (86 Stat. 532, Public Law 92-381).

63. State and Local Fiscal Assistance Act of 1972 (86 Stat. 919, Public Law 92-512, Oct. 20, 1972).

64. Rehabilitation Act of 1973 (87 Stat. 355, Public Law 93-112).

65. Domestic Volunteer Service Act of 1973 (87 Stat. 394, Public Law 93-113).

66. Comprehensive Employment and Training Act of 1973 (87 Stat. 839, Public Law 93-203).

67. Health Services Research, Health Statistics, and Medical Libraries Act of 1974 (88 Stat. 362, Public Law 93-353).

68. Safe Drinking Water Act (88 Stat. 1660, Public Law 93-523).

69. Indian Self-Determination and Education Assistance Act (88 Stat. 2206, Public Law 93-638).

70. National Health Planning and Resources Development Act (88 Stat. 2225, Public Law 93-641).

71. Headstart, Economic Opportunity, and Community Partnership Act of 1974 (88 Stat. 2291, Public Law 93-644).

72. Special Health Revenue Sharing Act of 1975 (89 Stat. 304, Public Law 94-63).

73. Developmentally Disabled Assistance and Bill of Rights Act (89 Stat. 486, Public Law 94-103).

74. Public Works Employment Act of 1976 (90 Stat. 999, Public Law 94-369).

75. Energy Conservation and Production Act (90 Stat. 1125, Public Law 94-389).

76. Indian Health Care Improvement Act (90 Stat. 1400, Public Law 94-437).

77. Health Professions Educational Assistance Act (90 Stat. 2243, Public Law 94-484).